# A Joyful Pause

# Nicole Taylor

# A Joyful Pause

## 52 ways to love life

For information about this title or to order other books and/or electronic media, contact the publisher:

Nicole Taylor
ajoyfulpause.com
info@ajoyfulpause.com

Library of Congress Control Number: 2018905471

ISBNs:
Print: 978-1-7322951-0-0
eBook: 978-1-7322951-1-7

Printed in the United States of America

*To my father, who likes baking cookies with his kids.*

# Contents

CONTENTS

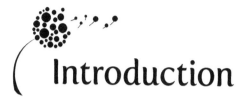

# Introduction

"... we cannot leave a part of us outside our love
if we would know our Self."
— *A Course in Miracles*

*T*his book is a love letter. It's a love letter to you, to the teachers who have lit the path, and to that Divine spark in each of us that we sometimes remember and sometimes don't, but who is there always, nonetheless.

This book is a love letter to love.

When we are in our most expansive state of being, we don't have to do anything to experience that fountain of love that is in us and that is us. But for many of us, this state of being flits in and out of our awareness. We may notice it during some sort of sublime experience: a gorgeous hike, a moment with a loved one, or in the midst of being creative. We want to feel constantly connected to this experience of eternal love. But, sometimes, we forget how to access that experience.

Why? Perhaps one reason is that our attention is constantly flowing out, and we aren't being encouraged to flow our attention back in. Our internal landscape creates how we see the world. So when we don't nurture and love ourselves, it is harder to act with kindness and love as we move through the world. If you haven't fed your heart, it will be hard to feed someone else's. We have forgotten how to come home to ourselves. Perhaps we were never taught how. And because of that gap in knowledge and in feeling, what often passes for rejuvenation or self-care is actually a kind of numbing behavior. The practices that actually restore body and mind, and connect back to spirit, take time, a bit of quiet, and some self-reflection.

Imagine you have a beautiful home. But instead of living inside, you set up a broken-down shack outside with whatever leftover things you can find. You set this shack up right there on the lawn of your beautiful home. You can't seem to find the key to your beautiful home, which now feels unfamiliar to you. You no longer know how you'd be comfortable there.

Taken literally, that scenario sounds completely illogical, and yet this is the struggle that many of us face as it relates to being at home with ourselves. Many of us end up opening the door to our beautiful abode and coming home to ourselves after a great wind comes and blows away that shack on the lawn. Usually the catalyst is some form of loss or transition—a love, a dream, a relationship. These experiences are devastating, like a great gust of wind that blows away life as we know it.

A loss or transition such as this brings with it a halt to the momentum of life. A natural pause emerges. Within that pause, all of the transient or changeable ways you've defined yourself are gone. Despite the pain of that transformation, you realize you still have a connection to something deep inside of yourself. This connection to the deep, eternal aspect of yourself is like a bright light in a dark place. It's the beacon that calls you home. It's the ground from which you remember that there is a love that resides in your heart that never dies. From that ground, you begin to heal.

We yearn for this experience of love and connection, for a feeling of being at home with ourselves. Our current epidemic of busyness temporarily keeps this yearning at bay, but staying busy for the sake of not feeling that yearning does not address the cause. In fact, busyness only increases our sense of disconnection and separation.

The connection we seek is in the pause. In moments of stillness, when we turn our awareness inward, we begin to approach that connection with our innermost selves, with the divine being in our hearts. Through that connection, we come to know that *we are home*.

I wrote this book to share the ways in which I have learned, over years of seeking home, to find that in myself.

# My Joyful Pause

$\mathcal{F}$ive years ago, I turned my life upside down. I created a situation in which the trajectory that I was on completely changed. While it was liberating, in some ways, to feel like I was starting over, I also felt deeply unsettled. I'd fallen asleep in life; I didn't realize it, and waking up was shocking. It was a wake-up call—a time for me to remember myself. So I embarked on a personal journey of self-remembrance little by little, day by day. In that time, I remembered how to be my own friend.

By grace, my seeking led to three different practices, all of which combined to give me an actual experience along the journey of self-love rather than an intellectual understanding of the importance of it. The practice of yoga in the Himalayan Tradition, the practice of Ayurveda, and the principles of Conscious Living all conspired to weave together to lead to the felt experience of deep self-care.

Yoga in the Himalayan Tradition takes into account more than how we currently think of yoga in the U.S., which is predominantly about the physical practice. In the Himalayan Tradition, the physical practice is part of a larger science that is about using everything at our disposal in service of our ultimate spiritual fulfillment and freedom.

Ayurveda is a 5,000-year-old science that uses yoga as a medicine to help move us toward balance. Ayurveda is the science of life, and it teaches us how to understand our true nature. Once we understand the nature with which we came into this world, we can adjust our daily routine, our nutritional habits, and the way we use our mind and senses in order to move closer to our dharma (our true purpose and reason for being here).

Conscious Living is about building presence through awareness of body, awareness of emotion, and awareness of thought. It's about loving where we are, right now, the way it is now. And through that acceptance, we can choose what we want to create and then take the next specific action available to get there.

These three streams taught me the value of humans tending to our own hearts. And there's no point at which we are "done." Self-love is a journey. I've stopped buying into the "myth of arrival"—the story we tell ourselves that there is an end point we are trying to reach. We think, "You love yourself, and *poof!* That's it—you remain in that state forever." But, just as love *between* people is a journey that ebbs and flows, so it is with loving ourselves. We are relearning constantly the practices of self-love. Life presents experiences that show where your love has not yet reached, and then your work is to rise up and flow love there. It isn't helpful to think of self-love as a destination, but rather as a practice that we are constantly engaging in daily.

I found that coming home to myself was a process that required making time each day to *pause*. To my surprise, in that pause, I often found a pulsing sense of joy. Whether that joy shined on its own or was mixed with some other emotion really didn't matter. Consciously creating and attending to the pause became the way I rebuilt my relationship to myself, the way I knew I was okay, no matter what was happening outside of me. The practices I'd learned of body awareness, meditation, yoga, and Ayurveda all coalesced into a practice I could do every day to help me remember my true nature.

Joyful pauses are available to all of us. The 52 practices I offer here are simple ways that I have used to help me remember that I am home. When done with full presence—and with a pause for breath and inner awareness after the practice—I experience a sense of internal warmth, love, and contentment so palpable it feels like it's in the space around me and inside of me. My hope is that, as you try these practices on, you also experience that enveloping sense of love and support.

## Why Pause?

By touching the sacred in ourselves daily, we are moved to a way of being in the world that inspires others to get in touch with that light in themselves.

When I pause, open myself up to my internal home space, and take a few breaths to rest there each day, I feel kinder, more available to connect with others, more excited about doing my work in the world, and ready to meet life with open arms. When I rest in my inner home, in the divine love that was placed in me by virtue of being born, it is easier to experience the pulse of spirit in everything around me. As you make this a practice in your own life, I imagine you'll find that the same ripple effect occurs.

Even if we have forgotten how, we can relearn simple ways to get in touch with that light that is always within us but is sometimes so covered up that we forget it's there. The good news is, just because we were taught to leave the lights off in our beautiful home doesn't mean we can't learn to flip the light switch on. The pages in this book provide you with 52 ways to turn on the light. My hope is that these practices help you to feel more at home in yourself, remember your inner illumination, and experience the value of spending some time in that lighted inner home every day.

These practices for coming home to yourself are stepping stones that are accessible to anyone, regardless of background, worldview, personal philosophy, or religion. They require no dogma. Because of my spiritual practice, these joyful pauses are shared in the context of each of us being connected through divine consciousness. I acknowledge that we all have different beliefs, but regardless of the particulars, everyone can pause, take a breath, and get present. If the word "divine" makes you feel uncomfortable, feel free to replace it with whatever word or feeling will allow you to take in the practice. In fact, you may find that these practices actually deepen your experience of spirituality, regardless of what form that takes.

These practices require only a willingness to build a track record of behaviors that will give you a direct experience of loving yourself. Within that willingness, I invite you to bring a stream of wonder that you can draw from when you feel challenged. Some of the suggestions may seem out of the ordinary to you, and it's that mixture of willingness and wonder that will keep your mind open and your heart engaged.

There is no difference between the sacred and the activities of daily living. Yes, you can sit on a meditation cushion every morning, or go to church, temple, or mosque, or other formal methods of engaging with spirit. But you can also make a meal with love and presence, or give to someone in need, or feel the divine in every step of your hike, or appreciate your beloved as the divine consciousness that they embody. We don't have to split things into "sacred" and "mundane."

We can live as if they are one, because they are. The act of creating joyful pauses with breath and present-moment awareness is the path to experiencing the sacred in everything. This inner revolution changes how we treat ourselves, which, in turn, is reflected in how we treat others.

The poet Rumi wrote, "What you seek is seeking you." When we take time to pause, we allow peace and harmony to meet us in that spaciousness. Your inner home wants to be occupied, and your inner light wants to be known. As you start to take on these practices, I invite you to hold the intention of willingness to be met by love. Because you are seeking the source of love, it's on its way. In truth, it's already here. These practices just help you remember.

## How It Works

There are three tools you'll need in order to undertake this journey.

+ Fire
+ Self-study
+ Surrender

In my decade of studying yoga, I learned that, when an action is imbued with these three elements, that action leads us back to feeling centered in ourselves and to experiencing an awareness of the consciousness that connects us all. Taking the joyful pauses found within these pages gave me direct experience of the power of fire, self-study, and surrender.

What's fire? It's the energy of transformation. As you undertake these joyful pauses, the fire of discipline will enable you to make time for them, despite your busy schedule. The fire of creativity will enable you to find ways to adapt these suggestions to your lifestyle. And the fire of courage will enable you to do even the ones that feel like a bit of a stretch.

What's self-study? It's our ability to observe ourselves—to understand our nature, beyond our habits, beyond our likes and dislikes, beyond the ways we automatically react or respond. Self-study is part of this journey in the form of the Journal Contemplations at the end of each joyful pause. I invite you to take the time to reflect on what you're experiencing.

What's surrender? It's trusting the process. It's letting these practices, plus time, help you remember your essence. It's letting go of a need to control. It's being willing to open up to new ways of seeing yourself and to let go of patterns that keep you feeling stuck and disconnected. It's realizing that, by releasing some of your attachment to your patterning, you can open up to more love and more connection.

Commit to doing these practices in whatever frequency is sustainable for you. The book is organized so that if you practice one pause per week (for as many days as you can that week), by the end of a year, you will have a demonstrated track record of making time in your life for self-care.

If we are trying to build a new muscle, that can only happen through repetition. I find I can maintain a state of curiosity and wonder when I encounter each of these practices as an experiment. With an experiment, you may have a hypothesis as to how it will turn out, but you are open to observing the result.

We can approach making time for joyful pauses in a similar manner. The intention is to make space for and take action to experience being at home in yourself. As you do each practice, have the intention to rest in your inner home, while also remaining open to exploring how each practice makes you feel. What is the result of the alchemy of doing the method, pausing afterward, breathing deeply, and drawing your awareness inward?

Home is where your spirit is, and home is within you wherever you go. It's easy to forget this, because, habitually, we place our awareness outside of ourselves. This tendency might be where resistance comes in as you begin these practices. You may not have much experience with consciously drawing your awareness in. And at first, you might not be comfortable with it. If that happens, just know that, like weight training, we are building new strength in muscles that haven't been used much. Between smartphones and the Internet, we have mountains of practice joining our minds with tantalizing sensory input. The practices in this book will help to create new mental muscles for drawing inward and coming home to yourself. Once you rest more in your inner home, you'll want to make it comfortable. These activities help you create an inner space that you love. Your constant companions of willingness and wonder will ensure that the home you learn to rest in feels warm, safe, and loving.

Any time we approach ourselves as "something to fix," we have no fun because we are giving ourselves the message that there is something wrong and that we aren't okay. Don't forget to have fun! We can approach these 52 practices as a celebration of who we are, and a liberation of some light we get glimpses of but would like to know more deeply. The process of coming home to yourself can be fun and enlivening.

If you find yourself using the practices to judge or critique yourself, notice this, and then come to a full stop. Be present with the emotions or thoughts that have arisen. Place your hands over your heart, and take some deep breaths into that space, until you feel a sense of inner tenderness begin to flow. Then, return to the practice. We are not trying to override any feelings or thoughts, but we do want to add new ones that are loving and kind and full of self-acceptance. I have found that, over time, the balance shifts, and the default becomes befriending ourselves rather than self-judgment. The mental image that comes to my mind is one of holding my own hand rather than letting it go. This process of sticking by your own side rather than abandoning yourself provides you with the felt sense of love—from you to you, and then rippling out to those around you.

Direct experience is our greatest teacher. You may find that the pauses within seem simple and you may already do some of them on your own. If so, that's great! The uniqueness and the utility of these practices comes from the pause and your experience of the pause. The infusion of breath, your ability to turn toward stillness, and your willingness to be fully present with your experience exactly as it is—that's what makes the joyful pauses transformative. When we add in the contemplations, so that you can reflect on your direct experience, we have a recipe for change that can penetrate our very being.

## The Intention

My intention is that each of the joyful pauses presents an opportunity for you to rest in your amazingness—and that, by making more time to rest in that amazingness, you feel connected to the energy that runs through everyone and everything.

May these 52 practices help you to remember that you are always home, you are always loved, and you are always light. May your journey with these practices help you to create the habit of making time to be in sacred space, which is as close as your intentional breath and deep presence.

# Put on your favorite song, and have a dance party with yourself

"The only thing that can solve most of our problems is dancing."
—*James Brown*

Forget all your stories about dancing. Let go of lamenting that you have no rhythm or that you move with two left feet. For those of you with training, I encourage you to release your attachment to the story of studying at Bladdy Blah Dance School under the esteemed Mrs. Danceypants. Leave all of your associations with the word "dance" at the door.

Put on a song.

Move to it.

Let's go into our mental computer and unhook "dance" from "the ability to execute choreography," or "looking like you know what you're doing when you move your body to music." Done? Good. You've released your inner dancer.

If you can move any part of your body, you can dance. Even if the only part of your body willing to move is your toe, move it in a way that only you can. That's the beauty of dance. We are each gifted with a unique form of expressing how we feel at any given moment. When we allow ourselves to dance, we invite our body to communicate what's true for us in that moment. We like to think of our mind as separate from our body, but they are one. The body has the same natural intelligence that informs the mind.

Dancing is a way to express what we don't have words for just yet. It is liberation. The imprints of our thoughts and emotions are stored within our muscles and other tissues. Think about the last time you felt scared—did you feel an accompanying tightening of your belly? When you get angry, does your jaw tighten? We've all heard someone say they have a lump in their throat when they feel sad. And as Shakira taught us, back in the early '00s, when we feel sexual, our hips don't lie. Our bodies are constantly communicating with us, and when we dance, we create a pathway for thoughts and emotions to move through.

During a period of time in my life when I was sitting in a stew of grief and guilt, my favorite song had a haunting, slow, stripped-down sound over guitar music that slowly built into a celebration of life. I felt like my insides were linked to the music, which gently built up in intensity until the singer sang, "Thank God I'm alive!" After that wave of ecstasy crested, her voice would take me back into still waters, which were somehow easier to wade in.

As I listened to her song, I moved with my sadness, feeling every inch of it through my breath. The slow, undulating, rhythmic movements that rose up through my hips broke up the feeling of "stuckness" inside and also created a smooth cycle that my breath easily began to follow. By the time she sang, "Thank God I'm alive," I was right there with her, having presenced my grief and gained some experience of the energy behind it, which was gratitude. I felt appreciation for life, for a comfortable home in which to dance, for being able to move my body, for the catharsis that music brings, and for an opportunity to accept life as it was in that moment. All of that from four minutes of dancing in my living room.

When we dance, we shift from one state to another. It doesn't matter if the song is fast or slow, joyful or contemplative. There's a beginning, a middle, and an end, and moving with it gives you the felt experience of the beginning, middle, and end of the energy you're choosing to express through your body. Whether that energy is an emotion or a desire you recently realized, when you dance, you're present when the wave of feeling rolls in and when it rolls out. Dancing with what's true for you gives you the opportunity to see your experience through to completion, just like listening to a song from beginning to end. When the clutter of unexpressed and unacknowledged thoughts and feelings are given expression through movement, you've cleared a space for yourself.

Done dancing for your four-minute song? Now turn off the music, and sit or lie down. For a few minutes, let your breath deepen, and rest a while in this new space. This is the beginning of creating space for yourself in your home.

## Journal Contemplations

- Where do you feel more spacious in your body after dancing?
- How does the quality of your breath change?
- Were there any parts of your body that you felt scared to move, and can you visualize your breath going to those places and soothing them?

# 2

## Bathe yourself leisurely, using products that delight your senses

"There must be quite a few things that a hot bath won't cure,
but I don't know many of them."
—*Sylvia Plath*

*A* beautiful way to build a relationship with your own heart is to take something that you do every day and infuse it with sacredness. When you bathe yourself leisurely, using products that delight your senses, it's a trifecta move: you're slowing down, you're giving your body loving attention, and you're soothing your senses. The multitasker in me loves this simple and meaningful method for starting off the day feeling deeply at home within.

Think back to your last shower or bath—did you rush through it, in a sort of autopilot way? Most of us can relate, and yet, it still happens. How you start the day often sets the tone for how you move through the rest of it. When you link a daily morning activity to moment-to-moment awareness and a slow pace, it's a sweet relief to your nervous system, which will be oh-so-grateful not to start the day in fight-or-flight mode.

The leisurely pace also creates room for you to give your body loving attention. How often is there time to just appreciate your body? When I rush bathing in the morning, I just want to get in and get out because I'm already thinking of all I have to do afterward. It isn't enjoyable, because I'm not present. When I stop and I notice, "Okay, I'm mentally already at the office rather than right here in the shower," I stop my momentum, close my eyes, and take a few deep breaths. I pay attention to the sensation of the water streaming onto my body. I relax my body into the heat and steam. I place the essential-oils scented soap near my nose and breathe in deeply. As I slow myself down, I climb down out of my head and actually experience my body, taking time as I bathe to appreciate my vitality, my strength, and my softness. I appreciate the parts of my body that I see as beautiful, and then I breathe waves of appreciation into those parts of my body that I find harder to accept. Truly, it's an act of self-love to take time to feel gratitude for the vehicle that houses your consciousness and allows your consciousness to experience the world.

Sensual experiences help us to luxuriate in the joy of life. What better way to open to the inherent beauty of life than to look for it in simple pleasures? When you create experiences of beauty for yourself as often as you can, you train your mind to keenly observe and even seek out the beautiful. We all have mental filters that are informed by events in our lives and our habits. We can cultivate mental filters for beauty, but it takes practice because the current habit is probably to notice what isn't working. For many of us, the default is on the negative side. And yet, when we work with beauty, when we live in a context of noticing what is beautiful in this moment, we begin to change our brain.

I love how *A Course in Miracles* puts it: "What you see reflects your thinking." As we train our minds to see beauty, we begin to notice flowers where we didn't see them before . . . smiles from other people that perhaps, in the past, we looked right through. It isn't that we start living in Shangri-la. Life happens, and you don't always find the beauty of moments with ease. But if your mental filter is set to beautiful, when things happen that don't feel that way, it's a little bit easier to take because you've spent so much of your day reveling in resplendence. Slowly, you learn to see the beauty in things that once looked very different. Focusing on the light in you by slowing down, appreciating yourself, and tapping into beauty results in your ability to see the light in everything else.

After your bathing ritual is complete, lie down on your bed, and take a few deep belly breaths. Let the soft caress of your own presence wash over you.

## Journal Contemplations

- Did you feel any resistance to slowing down your morning bathing, and, if so, where did you feel that in your body?
- How did you feel when you appreciated all of you—the parts of your body that aren't easy for you to love, as well as the parts that are?
- Are you aware of how your mental filter is usually set? In what ways could you shift it to include more beauty?

# 3

## Start your day by reading yourself a poem written by a mystic or a visionary

"Be patient toward all that is unsolved in your heart,
and try to love the questions themselves, like locked rooms and like
books that are now written in a very foreign tongue.
Do not now seek the answers, which cannot be given you,
because you would not be able to live them.
And the point is, to live everything. Live the questions now.
Perhaps you will then gradually, without noticing it,
live along some distant day into the answer."
—*Rainer Maria Rilke*

Mystical poets like Rainer Maria Rilke and Meister Eckhart had a beautiful way of using language to bridge form and formlessness. When you start your day in the presence of mystics and visionaries through their writing, you start your day by touching the infinite. Each morning, spending time with the words of those who experience an expanded consciousness can help us feel the divine as we move through the world.

It is easy for life to become a giant to-do list. I have found that when I don't invite mystical energy into my life, my experience is more flat and ho-hum. As I do the work of keeping my life on track and maintaining relationships, sometimes I get run down, and when I look at my full calendar, I wonder why I took all of this on in the first place. When the disconnect between our actions and our life purpose (dharma) gets wider, life can feel like a series of obligations.

Mystics remind us of spirit without the container of religion. They offer a vision that helps us see deeper into our experience. Remembering the infinite daily can help us reestablish the link between our actions and our purpose. While we each have our individual life's purpose and path to fulfillment, a shared purpose for all humans is to love. We work because we love, we play because we love, we shuttle our children around because of love, we give our full presence to our beloved even when we are tired because we love, and we even argue in a misguided request for love.

Contemporaries like Mary Oliver and David Whyte remind us of love. They call forth our connection to our source and our purpose in human life. Their writing can remind us of core values such as peace, connection, kindness, love of nature, and oneness. The consciousness that they usher us into is one of reclaiming our fullness. This is the work of integration, to embody the will to do what needs to be done while also understanding there is much that is beyond our control. Mystics invite us to see that there's no separation between the spiritual and the mundane. Their creative expression helps us to remember that every bit of experience is drenched in the all-pervading consciousness that pulses through all existence. That same consciousness animates us and allows us to observe our experiences without identifying with the way we feel about them. When we slow down and come home to ourselves, we tap into that deeper state of consciousness.

Rumi reminds us that our purpose can be found only by going inward when he writes, "Everyone has been made for some particular work, and the desire for that work has been put in every heart." Reading the words of someone who has done this inner work can put us in touch with the deep parts of our own hearts, where we find our inner teacher.

Let these mystics guide you into communing with that place in you that is love and truth and light. Allow your actions, through this remembrance, to rejoin with their purpose.

Feel your breath slow down and your body soften as you read the words that help you remember you are more than just this body. As your breath deepens, your body relaxes, and your mind quiets, having walked across this poetic bridge, you usher yourself into a place of deep silence. Let that silence penetrate your being, as you rest deeply, wanting nothing, having drunk from the well of remembering the part of you that has no beginning and no end. Rest here, in your true home, which is within you.

## Journal Contemplations

* How do you integrate your inner mystic with the aspect of your personality that's more concrete?
* In what ways does opening to mystical energy impact how you experience the events of your day?
* What role does art play for you in touching the infinite?

# 4

## Laughter is heart medicine. Train your mind to find the humor in daily life

"If you wish to glimpse inside a human soul and get to know a man,
don't bother analyzing his ways of being silent, of talking,
of weeping, of seeing how much he is moved by noble ideas;
you will get better results if you just watch him laugh."
—*Fyodor Dostoyevsky*

*T*hink of the last time you had a belly laugh. Did you feel a sense of warmth flowing through your body? Did an open, bright, sparkly feeling start in your chest and spread toward your extremities? Did your mood expand upward until you felt like you were flying? Laughter is heart medicine. At a physiologic level, we can feel the benefits: our breath flows with more ease, our bodies relax, and even the sensation of laughter is enjoyable. These benefits include the mind and heart as well—studies show that people who tend to find humor in situations have lower incidence of heart disease.

Humor reminds us of our wholeness. I remember when I was a resident advisor in undergraduate school. One of the students who loved to hang out in my room was blind. She had a razor-sharp sense of humor, and the first time I heard her crack a joke about not being able to see, I stopped in my tracks like a deer in headlights. She burst into laughter and poked me, cajoling me to laugh with her. In that moment, I realized that I treated her like she was breakable, but she wasn't. My perception was incorrect. She was whole and happy, and her energy said, "I'm working with what I've got." Whenever I have felt a glimmer of "inner woe-is-me," I have thought of Jessica and how she was gifted at both seeing her own wholeness and her ability to laugh at whatever life brought her.

One of the best feelings in the world is to share a deep laugh with someone that you love. Laughter is connection. It's levity. It's an expression of the sheer bliss of being alive in this body, at this time. Most children don't have a hard time laughing. The sense of innate joy is so close to the surface that, at the slightest reason, they will let loose an authentic, deep belly laugh. We may no longer be children, but we can give ourselves permission to return to the unbridled enjoyment that is a good belly laugh. We came into our bodies to experience consciousness in individual form. Why wouldn't we want to live into the humor that arises in everyday life?

It's possible that we shut ourselves down. In certain settings, such expressions of joy are viewed as inappropriate, and a sense of gravitas translates socially as maturity, while mirth translates as lacking the depth to be taken seriously. Rather than succumb to social conditioning, try living more into your sense of humor, and feel the medicine that laughter brings. It's okay if you give yourself a boost—watch a comedian or read a humor writer or some satire (*The Onion* always provides a giggle). When you start to seek humor, it finds you.

After a good laugh, observe the sensations in your body. Notice the upward-moving energy in your chest. Breathe into that space, and luxuriate in the delicious feeling there. According to yogic philosophy and energetic anatomy, at the subtler levels of our existence, the part of our awareness closest to our soul is the bliss body. Laughter gives us a peek into the light and joy that is closest to our true nature.

## Journal Contemplations

+ The next time you stifle a laugh, notice the thoughts that are present. What stories dampen your experience of expressing your joy?
+ After a good laugh, notice your sense of well-being. For you, how does laughter help you to feel into your wholeness?
+ When you drop into the energy behind the laughter, how do you experience being connected to your deepest Self?

# 5

# See the world through
# your beauty glasses

"Never lose an opportunity of seeing anything beautiful,
for beauty is God's handwriting."
—*Ralph Waldo Emerson*

*W*hat is beauty to you? Do you see it as the underlying aspect of everything seen and unseen? Are you open to experiencing your own inner and outer beauty? When I have a hard time experiencing beauty, I have found it helpful to appreciate the beauty outside of me as a way to come into a space of relating to the world as a beautiful place. One core principle of Ayurveda is that everything found in the body is also found in the universe. The same beauty that I get in touch with through delighting in a bouquet of flowers is in me as well. One of the core values seen by the yogis is that the world is beautiful because it is a manifestation of the Divine. Part of the reason we sometimes feel disconnected from the inner fountain of beauty is that we feel disconnected from our divine source. In reality, we are never disconnected from that source, but our experience of it waxes and wanes, based on the quality of our consciousness.

It is up to us to curate what we allow into our world and what we don't. When we are watching, reading, and talking about things that make us feel the world is a dark and unsafe place, we start to view the world through that lens. And when we fill our consciousness with beauty, we see the world through that lens. As we know from experience in life, in truth, both exist: horrible things happen, and also love abounds. It's important to be able to be present with both. This is the paradox of living. Being able to see beauty lets us experience the world and everything in it as whole rather than broken.

We seek beauty, not to suppress our feelings when things that are hurtful do occur, but rather, to enjoy life as it is. We seek beauty to seed the ground to be able to bear witness to our pain and the pain of others while maintaining an inherent awareness of the intrinsic divinity that underlies all creation. That intrinsic beauty is always there and is available to us when we are in the present moment.

One day I spoke with a friend who was feeling guilty about an intense fight she'd had with her niece, in which they'd said some harmful things to each other. She was so distraught about the fight that she went to her mother and lay her head on her mother's shoulder. She said her mother comforted her so tenderly and that she hadn't experienced that level of support from her mother since she'd been a small child. The disagreement, which seemed painful and dark, also had the power to bring more light into a different relationship. The light that was underneath the darkness is, to me, the manifestation of that inherent beauty that permeates everything.

How can you step into this space? Perhaps it's making sure your home feels beautiful and comfortable to you. Maybe you love to dress up, or perhaps you have a way that puts you in touch with your inner beauty. It could be getting out into nature and the beauty of the outdoors. Maybe it's relaxing into the *is-ness* of this moment, with deep presence and acceptance. Whatever your method is, after you step into that space of appreciating beauty, pause. Breathe into the inherent beauty of all things. And know that the source of beauty is in you.

## Journal Contemplations

- How do you experience fullness and beauty in your daily life?
- What is your particular way of contributing to the beauty in the world?
- How does your speech impact your experience of beauty?

# 6

## At the end of each day, write down or say aloud an appreciation for yourself

"The deepest craving of human nature is the need to be appreciated."
—*William James*

According to *Harvard Business Review*, the highest-performing teams have a ratio of almost six appreciations given for every criticism. When you think of the way that you talk to yourself, what's your ratio of appreciations to criticisms? As the head of the team of your body, senses, breath, mind, and wisdom, are you contributing to keeping your team performing well?

One way to increase your appreciation ratio daily is to start and end the day with an appreciation for yourself. I once stayed with a beautiful yogini who taught me this practice. Each night before bed, she would snuggle into herself and share appreciations for me and then for herself, and I'd do the same. The quality of my sleep was amazing that week, as I went to bed basking in positive regard. I invite you to try it!

We can think of the mind as a crystal. When we forget our true nature and start to identify with the roles we play in life, our likes, our dislikes, our fears, or changeable qualities like thoughts and emotions, a film begins to obscure the clarity of the crystal. Practices such as journaling, meditation, prayer, and contemplations of spiritual texts help to clear the mind of the debris of false identification with such changeable states. As the mind gets clear, the light of the soul shines through with more ease, and that light informs how we experience ourselves and the world.

Placing appreciation in your mind before bed helps you to reconnect to your inner light—the clarity and harmony that is the mind resting in its true nature. As you are more aware of your inner light, you're more able to see the good in others. Your recognition of the good, beautiful, loving, and light that you are makes your mind naturally see and appreciate those qualities outside of yourself. And your ability to presence your own darkness also helps, as you learn to be with your shadow characteristics without identifying with them, which, in turn, allows you to learn from whatever they have to teach you.

Additionally, nighttime is the right time to clear away the mental debris of the day. Many of us cap off the day by filling our minds with stimulating images from the Internet or television, and this stimulation has an impact on the quality of our sleep. That type of sensory input has the same effect on your mind as something very spicy has on your stomach. Ending your day with appreciation is to your mind what soothing chamomile tea is to your belly.

If you are in a relationship, sharing appreciation before bed is also a juicy way to create intimacy with your beloved. Wouldn't you delight in knowing what your partner appreciates about themselves? I feel excited thinking about hearing my Love appreciate his amazing qualities. While getting to sleep takes a little longer with the added time it takes to appreciate yourselves and one another, surrounding each other with mutual respect and love is a great way to tend to your relationship daily.

Making space in your own heart and mind for appreciation is a key ingredient to learning to rest in your true nature. It's much easier to come home to yourself when you appreciate that home. The act of speaking it out loud or writing it down is the extra step of expression that amplifies the wave of appreciation. After you offer the appreciation, pause, breathe, and rest in the sense of inner sweetness that your expression has generated.

## Journal Contemplations

- Do you find it hard to appreciate yourself? If so, what are you telling yourself that is creating a struggle, and how can you relax and soften into seeing your own light?
- You can make a game out of appreciation. How many appreciations can you rack up for yourself during the day? You can apply this also to coworkers and your partner.
- One gift of the inner critic, which we all have, is that they miss nothing. Can you use that skill to miss no opportunity to appreciate the good in yourself or others?

# 7

# Slow down

"For fast-acting relief, try slowing down."
—*Lily Tomlin*

$\mathcal{S}$ometimes the simplest techniques are the most difficult to practice. As you read the words "slow down," you may be thinking, *Sure I'll slow down—and who is going to take care of this to-do list marching across my mind?* Yes, slow down. The choice to slow your own momentum is an integral part of coming home to yourself. How can you rest in your source if your body and mind are flitting from one thing to another, defining life only through what you do rather than who you are? Have you experienced what happens when you pause to notice the power in you that allows you to achieve these things? This sense of inner expansion and gratitude for that source arises when we pause.

We can get creative in how we find the time to slow down. When I've been sitting at my desk for a while at work and then get up to go to a meeting, I may take that opportunity to practice walking meditation to my meeting, noticing the feeling of one foot making contact with the ground as my other foot peels itself off of the ground. If I'm driving home from work, I may try to drive at an unhurried pace (a practice that takes real discipline when you live in a city!), in silence, so my mind can empty. I've come to understand that even though being really fast feels good to me, slowing down daily to get present is what keeps my battery charged enough to go fast when I need to. If I don't make time to pause, I go from 70 mph to sick or deeply fatigued. You may also be able to relate to busyness as a way to avoid big feelings. Slowing down allows for digestion of big feelings as they happen, rather than skipping over them and having them pop up in unconscious ways.

How can your lifestyle accommodate slowing down? Perhaps you make a commitment to slow down by leaving a few nights this week completely unscheduled. Turn your phone off, and for the evening treat your home as an exotic island inhabited only by you and anyone who lives with you. Slowing down is a mind-set that's about being present. It can be hard to be present when we are fleeing into the future by moving too quickly or getting stuck from spending too much time looking back at the past.

When we slow down, we don't come to a halt, but we experience a shift from becoming to being. When we slow down, we choose to be here, consciously. It's important not to use slowing down to act in ways that are unconscious. For example, if you pick a day to leave unplanned, but then you fill that day with activities that numb you out, then you've just succumbed to inertia. The difference between inertia and choosing to slow your pace is that the latter is informed by a high quality of consciousness and presence, so that you can feel connected to the source in you that powers your actions.

In whatever manner the slowing down comes to you, once you are there, pause. Feel that deep connection in your heart, that glimmering sense of contact with the part of you that is pure awareness. Feel how you fully inhabit your experience, all the way to the edges of yourself. Notice that your breath has deepened. Does a feeling of well-being pervade your awareness? Rest in that. You are home.

## Journal Contemplations

- As you slow down, any negative stories that you have about a slower pace will start to arise. How can you reframe slowing down in a way that supports your commitment to making more time for being?

- A hidden motivator for not slowing down can be thoughts or emotions that we are avoiding. If this happens for you, take a few moments to journal about it, or talk to a friend or counselor. How does the avoidance shift after you express the thoughts or feelings?

- Make a list of habits you have that are numbing. Can you discern the difference between these and choosing to slow your momentum?

# 8

## Set an alarm to remind you, three times a day, to take five belly breaths and come home to yourself

"In our more lucid moments, when we have quieted the hubbub
of our distractions, we are capable of sensing the power and
intelligence that sustain us and everything else.
In such moments, it is hard not to feel touched by the sublime,
by that which links all the things in the world together,
by the eternal essence that is at the heart of our existence."
—*Yogarupa Rod Stryker*

To master anything, we have to practice it. You wouldn't step onto a tennis court for the first time and expect to be Serena Williams, right? But when it comes to matters of self-development, many times we take that impatient approach with ourselves. Have you ever read a book or taken a workshop, gotten all fired up, only to come home and lose that passion and fire as soon as your regular life starts to take over again?

For me, this pattern began to change when I started to meditate. The alchemy of committing to sit on that cushion for a set amount of time each day, come hell or high water, taught me the value of practice. Not to say that I never find myself being distracted and scattered, but the practice of breath awareness makes it easier to notice and to adjust accordingly. It was only after I acquired that discipline that I became more adept at getting out of my own way.

Similarly, we can make coming home to ourselves a daily practice. As Malcolm Gladwell wrote in *Outliers*, it takes at least 10,000 hours of deliberate practice to approach mastery. Now think of how many times you breathe in an hour. So we will need to come home to ourselves at least that many times before the practice becomes as familiar to us as breathing or eating. Choosing to pause begins to flower when we start to weave it into the fabric of our day. One way to use technology to support you in this practice is to set an alarm on your phone to remind you, three times a day, to take five belly breaths and come home to yourself.

Deep breathing is one of the most accessible methods we have for returning our awareness inward. The simple act of belly breathing has a calming effect on your body and mind, helping your scattered mind draw back to itself and turn inward. If you're breathing deeply, five belly breaths will take about a minute. This minute-long pause can be enough to at least help you to notice your current state. Where is your awareness? Are you still being present with yourself, holding your own hand as you would a friend's? Or have you completely looped your awareness out to another person, place, or thing, and forgotten to pay attention to your inner experience?

At the end of the five rounds of belly breathing, place your awareness in the space around your heart, and get curious. Continue to bring your nonjudgmental awareness to how you feel. Don't be surprised if emotion crosses your mind. Stay present with that emotion without becoming identified with it. After this pause, return to your regular activities. Most likely, your experience will shift because you've refined the level of your presence.

Taking this pause throughout the day helps you start to cultivate this practice of returning home to yourself. While your meditation practice or other relaxation techniques have the same impact of returning your awareness inward, it is also important to take a pause and return home in the middle of a meeting, or as we ride the bus home, or as we eat lunch with a friend. We are showing ourselves that this home base is always available, and is just a deep breath or five away.

In my life, this pivotal practice shows me that I love myself enough to prioritize my connection with myself and my source. There is no goal, no person, no emotional state that supersedes my commitment to coming home to myself. When we give ourselves that level of commitment, we know that we truly value our inner home, and that love and value is the bedrock from which we build our lives.

## Journal Contemplations

- As you start this practice, notice: do you have a split in your mind between the spiritual and daily activities of living? How might you bring this sense of inner expansion into your life?
- As you make time in your day for centering, do you observe any shifts in your ability to focus?
- How does this practice impact your ability to be fully available for your life?

# 9

# Take a walk in Mother Nature, noticing Her bounty by focusing on the sounds, scents, sights, and textures She has to offer

"The clearest way into the Universe is through a forest wilderness."
—*John Muir*

According to Ayurveda, the ancient science of life and self-healing that originated in India, humans are a microcosm of the macrocosm that is the larger universe. The elements and energies found in the universe are also found in us. Just as the building blocks of our bodies are represented by the five elements of earth, water, fire, air, and space, those same five elements can be found in various permutations in Nature. If we look at our physical form and the physical form of the Nature, we can start to understand the relationship we have with the elements. We can think of the structure of our body as earth, just like Nature has soil, from which life grows. Our bodily fluids are water, much like Nature has oceans and rivers and rain. The heat and metabolism in our body can be seen as fire, similar to Nature's sun. Air flows into and out of our lungs, much like the wind moving through the trees in Nature. And the spaces in our bodies, from our nose, to our mouth, to our ears, mimics the space in Nature, which is the container for all that we experience.

It is easy to forget our own inner bounty as we identify with the roles we play in life, our likes, dislikes, thoughts, and fears. But Nature's beauty is so stark, so apparent, that exposure to Her can be a gateway to remembrance of our own true nature and inner luminosity.

Nature has Her own sense of stillness. Pulsing underneath the cacophony of animal sounds and the rustling of wind blowing through the trees is the sound of stillness. Her natural quiet can draw us into our own inner stillness.

Getting into Nature does not always require a three-hour hike in a forest, though that can be quite enjoyable. You can find a park or a grassy space close to your neighborhood. Take a walk, feeling each step invite you into your own presence more deeply. Notice the sound of your feet against the earth, the chirping of the birds, the rustle of the leaves on the trees. Breathe deeply into your belly, and let Nature's perfume wash through your cells. Let the natural sweet scent of the air bring you closer to your own sweetness. Let your eyes fill with the beauty of the way the sunlight filters through the trees, the unique elegance of each flower and plant, and the way the current season is being expressed through the landscape.

Get tactile and touch Nature. Dig your fingers into the dirt. Place your hands or your back against the bark of a tree. Touch the leaves of a plant (caveat: leaves of three, let it be). Pause here, breathing deeply. Let the beingness of Nature draw you into your own beingness.

One reason we have a hard time resting in ourselves is that we have lost touch with the eternal aspect of our nature and are identifying with the changeable aspect of ourselves. When we get our bodies and minds into natural settings, the eternal aspect of Nature can help draw us back to that eternal aspect within us.

We can find everything in Nature—from beauty, ugliness, and new life, to death, the smell of flowers, and the smell of animal feces. When we take a walk in Nature, we can have the experience of accepting all of these pairs of opposites, because we experience the harmony that pervades it all. I find that, after a walk in Nature, I feel more accepting of the different (and sometimes disparate) aspects of myself and others, and I feel closer to an experience of the underlying harmony that pervades everything, including my own being.

One time, I was on a hike with a guide named Bob Thomas, a volunteer for the Fairmount Park Conservancy. We were near Belmont Plateau in Philadelphia, and as he pointed out the nursery where the young trees live until they are ready to be planted, he said, "Here, the trees are raised in happiness."

I was so struck by that. For the remainder of the hike, the phrase "raised in happiness" reverberated through my mind. I wondered, *Am I raising myself in happiness?* Some days, it's more like I'm pickling myself in criticism. Whenever I notice that, I make a point to step into the woods, where I experience a relaxation of my nervous system, a softening of my body and breath, and I'm reminded of this idea of raising myself in happiness. How best can I care for myself? What can I connect to in me that creates deeper connections with others? In what ways can I cultivate peace?

When you prioritize being in Nature on a regular basis, you create the conditions that, no matter what happens as you move through your life, you'll have the opportunity to use Nature as the bridge back home to yourself.

# Journal Contemplations

- How does attending to the experience of your senses while you're in Nature impact how you feel?
- Can you notice how earth, water, fire, air, and space show up in Nature and how they show up in your own body?
- How do you experience the continuous cycle of creating, maintaining, and destroying in Nature and in yourself?

# 10

# Smile at a stranger, and breathe into the sense of connection between you

"Love, as your body experiences it, is a micro-moment of connection
shared with another. And decades of research now shows that love,
seen as these micro-moments of positive connection,
fortifies the connection between your brain and
your heart and makes you healthier."
—Barbara Fredrickson, PhD

At our core, we are love. I've learned from my teachers that the pulsation of expansion and contraction, which permeates the entire universe, is the pulsation of the desire to love and be loved. We were created in love. Love is the unifying force, the felt experience of the universality of consciousness that is the through-line of everything that exists.

One way that we make it hard to rest in ourselves is to cut off the stream of love that naturally flows through us. When we start to focus on what separates us rather than what joins us, we box ourselves in, partitioning our love by limiting our connections. We move through the world as if we have to protect ourselves from those who would see our openness as weakness.

In *Love 2.0*, researcher Barbara Fredrickson reframes the way we think of love. Rather than a constant state we work to maintain, she changes the context of love to one of micro-moments of connection. These micro-moments are available to us all of the time, but we may miss them because we have told ourselves we can connect only with people who are known to us. We reserve our openhearted connection for family or friends, perhaps out of a belief that it isn't safe to share a moment of connection with a stranger. Other times, we miss opportunities to connect with others because we are choosing to connect with our mobile device rather than the person in front of us. And yet, that impulse to share love is not being given Her full expression. Ignoring the natural uprising of love that occurs when we encounter another also hampers our ability to rest in that sense of love for ourselves. Slowly, the world feels disconnected and unsafe.

Luckily, we can shift from disconnection to connection. Just as our behavior created the feeling of separateness, we can use behavior to reopen the channels of connection.

Eye contact while smiling is one of the easiest ways to create connection. Of course, your smile and your desire to connect need to be authentic. Try this only when you genuinely feel open to connecting.

I would venture to say that expressing your joy at being in the presence of another person is one of the simplest forms of showing love. Whether this is shared with a stranger on the bus or someone you notice walking down the street, you're supporting that flow of love from you to others and back to yourself.

It is really easy to use the morning commute on public transportation as a way to get a head start on emails or surf the web, looking for a laugh. I found that, when I got to work, I would already be less interested in talking to people on the way in and more interested in getting back to my computer. After reading about micro-moments of connection, I figured I would put it into practice on the subway or the bus. I would be present, and breathe, and if I caught a friendly gaze, I would pause and smile. Sometimes the person would look away quickly, as in, *We are in a city, and we do not look at one another in the eye while smiling*. But most of the time, I shared a nice moment with a stranger. I remember a woman who looked like the sweetest grandmother, and we gazed at each other, open for connection. As I smiled at her, I could quite literally feel a sensation of spreading love and sweetness across my chest.

Are you willing to try it? You'll notice there's a natural arc of connection, sustaining, and letting go of the connection. After the moment of connection is over, pause, and take a few breaths to relax into your experience before moving on to the next thing. This sense of love and connection is your inner home. Lean into that place in yourself.

## Journal Contemplations

- What obstacles to connection do you notice arising when you make eye contact?
- Are there any fears of rejection that arise, and if so, how do you respond?
- As you create more room for connection in your day, is there any change in how you respond to challenges?

# 11

## Rub warm oil all over your body. Lie down, and be present with the sensations that arise

"By using oil massage daily, a person is endowed with pleasant touch, trimmed body parts and becomes strong, charming and least affected by old age."
—Charaka Samhita *Vol. 1, V: 88–89*

According to Ayurveda, the Indian science of living life in harmony with your true nature, self-massage supports balance, not only in your body but also in your mind. Self-massage (abhyanga) is an easy and nurturing way to come back home to yourself. In my life, this began an internal revolution. When I first started learning about Ayurveda, I was very comfortable in my head, thinking and analyzing as a way to keep some distance between myself and the world. I wasn't completely disconnected from my body, but I found that I wasn't very aware of the wisdom it held, either, since I placed a higher value on intellect. When I began studying with Kathryn Templeton and started working with Ayurveda, abhyanga was the practice I wanted to do the least. It was messy. I felt that it took a long time. I had a ton of resistance to it. But I stuck with it and started to notice how deliciously cared for I felt on the days that I did abhyanga and how my inner reserves of patience and kindness seemed a bit lower on the days that I didn't. Abhyanga was the practice that gave me direct experience of what flight attendants mean when they tell you to put the oxygen mask over your own face before putting it on someone else's. By creating time for this self-nurturing, I actually had more to give. And when I didn't do it for a few days, I noticed I felt less willing to give, less patient, less available, because inside I needed nurturing and care. Every person I have taught this to has had a different and deep experience of the gifts of self-massage.

To enter into this timeless self-care ritual, you'll need a dry wash-cloth or a dry brush, a cup of warm oil, some clothes, and a blanket that you don't mind getting oily. If you tend to run hot, use coconut oil. If you tend to run cold and your skin is often dry, use sesame oil. If you tend to run cool and your skin is not usually dry, use sweet almond or sunflower oil.

Take the dry washcloth or dry brush, and sweep it down your body from top to bottom, moving the washcloth/dry brush up and down the limbs and body to create heat, activate lymph flow, and slough off dead skin. Then massage yourself with the warm oil, using long strokes on muscles and circles on joints. Rub your face with oil, and don't forget to massage your fingers and toes, scalp, and ears.

As you do the massage, let your mind fill with appreciation for the moment. If you'd like to deepen the experience, breathe diaphragmatically, so that, as you inhale, the belly fills with breath, and, as you exhale, it empties. After you feel comfortable doing so, listen to the sound of the breath. The natural mantra that rides the breath is "So" on the inhalation and "Hum" on the exhalation. So Hum means "I am That" and the mantra is a bridge between our individual experience and the universal consciousness that pulses through everything. Breathe in "So," and breathe out "Hum" while you do abhyanga.

When you're finished, rest. Lie down on your blanket comfortably, and breathe diaphragmatically. During this pause, be present with yourself. Notice the sensations that arise, and let your mind melt into them. Feel into the support you've created for improved circulation, for the impurities in your body to release into the oil, and for the healing touch you've offered yourself through this practice.

Allow the physical sensations to become more attractive to your mind than your thoughts. Let them capture your mind, leading you to a place where there is just space—space that leads to a sense of inner peace and deliciousness that could only be the beginning of bliss, the layer of our awareness closest to the soul. That bliss is yours to claim, and it is only the beginning of what lies in you when you choose to come home to yourself.

After a few minutes, you can move into meditation or shower off the oil, and move mindfully into your day.

## Journal Contemplations

+ Did you find it hard to make time for this practice? What are your time-scarcity stories, and how did you overcome them?
+ What was your experience of being still after the self-massage?
+ How did you move through your day after taking time for abhyanga?

# 12

# Volunteer in your
# community

"What is the essence of life? To serve others and to do good."
—*Aristotle*

The easiest way to gain perspective on your personal suffering is to help someone else. At a very basic level, we are all
connected. In an episode of the show *Cosmos*, physicist Neil deGrasse
Tyson shared, "We are all made of star stuff." The same energy that
powered stars billions of light years away has the same building blocks
as the energy that powers our bodies. Our interconnectedness affords
us the ability to feel good when we help each other. For centuries, yogis
saw that selfless service was a path to enlightenment, as evidenced by
an entire branch of yoga called karma yoga. In this form of yoga, the
path to an experience of union is based in the actions we take to help
others, as we release our attachment to the fruits of those actions and
do all of our work in service to the Divine. The Buddhists have the idea
of the Bodhisattva, who delays her own enlightenment until all beings

are enlightened. And Jesus was an amazing example of being of service. All of the wisdom traditions have service as a part of their practice. And countless people who do not follow any particular spiritual path still make time to care for others.

Think of how you felt the last time someone asked for help and you assisted them. Did you feel a rush of energy or joy? By giving so freely, did you get in touch with the boundless resources within you? This is the gift of volunteerism.

Our true nature is one of fullness. Scarcity is of the mind. There are people who don't have much, but they are connected to their innate sense of fullness. However, without support, it can be easy to get run down and to feel as though there is not enough of us to go around. Getting out into the community and giving of ourselves reminds us that we do have these boundless internal resources. We have the felt experience of the interconnectedness between us all, and we see that, when we give of ourselves to the community, we receive that energy back in the form of feeling more connected to something bigger than ourselves.

According to *A Course in Miracles*, "To have, give all to all." Essentially this means that we don't really have anything until we give it to others. When we give love and service to others, we can recognize love in ourselves. And when we recognize love in ourselves, we have found our home.

I enjoy giving free classes to caregivers. There is something so delightful about teaching a free yoga class to people who spend their whole day doing amazing things for other people. There comes a moment in the class, during the last few reclining poses, when a sweet look of relaxation, surrender, and deep centering comes across the faces of the students. As the teacher, I feel honored to lead them through a practice that helps them to feel that way; I feel happy to help them create conditions to deeply feel their own inner flow of love. It reminds me that, no matter what I have going on, love is the priority—a love that flows inward and a love that flows outward into the world.

You can get creative with your giving. Local parks are often looking for volunteers to help them clean up. Beautifying your neighborhood can be a great way to give back.

Every day, find a way to give. This does not have to be monetary. It can be your time, your attention, your skills, and your love. Give what you can without regard for what you'll receive. And then relax into the feeling that arises in you after giving of yourself. Pause, and be with that feeling.

## Journal Contemplations

- What happened to your heart as you volunteered in your community?
- How did any feelings of separation change as you saw similarities between yourself and the other volunteers?
- Do you have a sense for the huge amount of love you have to share?

# 13

## Snuggle into your most comfortable chair, and read purely for fun

"A book, too, can be a star, a living fire to lighten the darkness,
leading out into the expanding universe."
—*Madeleine L'Engle*

The two key words for this way to come home to yourself are "snuggle" and "fun." When we think of snuggling, we usually think it takes two, but you can snuggle yourself just as well. In fact, it's important. A feeling of gathering yourself inward in a loving way can be extremely nurturing. We know there's a part of us that remembers that hugged-in feeling from being in the womb, and babies clearly remember it because they love being swaddled. I imagine snuggling into your most comfortable chair as a form of swaddling yourself. It's not that we are trying to regress to an earlier stage of life, but we are showing ourselves a sense of nurturing at a very palpable level. The physical manifestation of being hugged in, alerting our minds and hearts to a feeling of "I've got you" is a huge pull for our awareness.

Awareness wants to return to itself, so when we move in that direction with the body, feeling cozy and relaxed, we feel more ease with which to turn toward ourselves. In the very way we melt into a hug with a loved one, we can melt into ourselves. A soft blanket and a comfortable chair are all that's required. Having fun is equally important here. If we do all of the physical nurturing to set up a sense of being hugged internally and then we bombard our consciousness with negative images or stressful material, we set ourselves up for more feelings of separation rather than inner connectedness. For this exercise, put down the murder mystery, and instead choose something that is less intense for your senses. Whether it's fiction or biography or something spiritual, just make sure that what you're reading is like a hug for your mind rather than an agitation.

The action of physically supporting ourselves and bringing something pleasurable into the mind through reading moves us out of the energy of needing to do something and into the energy of just *being*. Being is our true nature—being is where our individual consciousness can come home to its source, and we can feel that internal sense of fullness. Whether your life has been marked by all of the hugs or whether you have felt quite isolated, your ability to comfort yourself, to create an internal space of safety and nurturing, is key to a continued sense of well-being.

There are many ways that we comfort ourselves, and not all of them are so helpful or even good for our health. Getting hugged in and reading might seem really simple, but so many of us are yearning for feeling deeply loved, and we reach for whatever is close that will help to settle our inner restlessness. Each time in my life that I have come into a state of transition, I have come face to face with my inner restlessness and the many unhelpful coping skills I have adopted in order to avoid the full feeling of that restlessness. In my snuggle-and-read sessions, I have parsed the difference between feeling lonely and being alone.

I'm reminded of a joke I heard by a comedian, in which he said the reason we constantly reach for our cell phones is that there is a dark hole of suppressed emotion and loneliness that we are avoiding, and when we have some space and time, like in our car at a stoplight, the pull of that emotion gets louder, and we have to pick up the phone to drown it out. Obviously, the way he tells it is funny and not sad like what I just wrote, but you get my drift. The snuggle-and-read is a way to be with whatever it is that we need to feel. Emotion will arise when we start to relax, but the hugged-in-ness of this moment can help us to sit with ourselves. (And what if the emotion is delight? That is an option, too). We don't have to reach for anything to take us out of our current state because we are holding our own hand while whatever it is that needs to flow through, does.

In reading, we are taken to new worlds. We experience things that haven't actually happened to us, and we see something about ourselves that we may not have seen if not for our experience of reading. After you've enjoyed your hugged-in reading session, pause. Take a moment to notice how you experience your own comfort. Breathe into that comfort, and know that a sense of well-being is yours whenever you want it.

## Journal Contemplations

+ How did you choose something uplifting to read? What did your mind naturally gravitate toward?
+ Do you have any resistance to taking time to create a sense of well-being for yourself?
+ How do you parse the difference between feeling lonely and the gift of solitude?

# 14

# Breathe into your emotions, and stay present until the waves pass

"An emotion like anger that's an automatic response lasts just ninety seconds from the moment it's triggered until it runs its course. One and a half minutes—that's all. When it lasts any longer, which it usually does, it's because we've chosen to rekindle it."
— *Pema Chodron*

Many of us have not learned how to be present with our emotions without feeling overwhelmed by them. That discomfort is part of why we find it hard to be with ourselves. When our home feels out of control to us, it makes sense that we wouldn't want to be there, right? If we learn how to build our emotional intelligence, we create a gateway to our being willing to rest in ourselves. It is much easier to deal with waves if you know how to surf them rather than feeling like you're drowning in the undertow.

There is plenty of research to suggest that an emotion lasts only a few seconds. It's what we add to the emotion that prolongs its existence.

If we have not learned that it's okay to feel sad, when sadness starts to flow through as energy in motion, we may contract around it and add fear. If we also haven't learned to presence fear, we may add distraction to avoid feeling either of those emotions. Distraction may look like picking up a drink, getting busy, spending time worrying, or becoming hypercritical. The full initiation, rising, crest, and outflow of the original emotion didn't happen smoothly once we added all of that mental debris. On a deep level, we experience the distractions we add as a kind of inner abandonment, similar to turning the water on, seeing it coming out of the faucet, and then running out of the house. Then the add-on emotion, which in the example above was fear, is like realizing the toilet is running, and, rather than lift the lid up to determine the reason, again, we leave the house with the toilet and faucet overflowing.

The more things that happen in this house that we refuse to presence, the more resistance we will have to coming home. We can turn this tide around by being willing to be with ourselves as these emotions arise. I learned from Kathlyn Hendricks that the core emotions are fear, anger, sadness, joy, and sexual feelings. The more we are able to stay with ourselves as these states pass through, the easier it is to rest in ourselves. From a yogic perspective, thoughts and emotions are waves that cross the ocean of the mind. Just as you wouldn't take action on every thought that crosses your mind, you don't need to react to every emotion that crosses your awareness. You can observe the emotion, just like you can observe thought or sensation in your body. And the observation and presence you bring to it is what allows the wave to flow through.

The key is the breath. Diaphragmatic breathing is a great way to bring presence to emotions. The next time you feel one of the core emotions arise, turn toward it with your awareness. Notice the accompanying body sensations. Initiate diaphragmatic breathing, and perhaps even visualize your breath going to the place where you feel the emotion. Keep your awareness purely on the sensation—not on any accompanying stories about the emotion. Bring your exquisite awareness to your experience until the emotion passes through. Pause, savoring your willingness to stay with yourself through your experiences.

Connecting to that awareness was like walking back into the house, turning off the faucet, and fixing the running toilet. This is your home, and you are ready to respond to what occurs in it instead of being at the effect of it.

Sometimes we find that giving ourselves permission to fully feel our emotions opens us to the spontaneous joy and sense of calm that underlies all experience. I have found a sweetness underneath sadness, a clarity underneath anger, an excitement underneath fear. None of this would've been possible to experience without first being willing to stay with myself as the initial feeling flowed.

We can experience our inner world as a castle, the place from which we draw strength to act in the world. Tending to our experience and giving ourselves the gift of presence is integral to building this inner power.

## Journal Contemplations

+ Were there emotions that were not okay for you to acknowledge feeling or expressing in your family? Are there any that you have an aversion to feeling?
+ How do you deal with those now?
+ Can you use the pause between noticing the emotion and reacting, then choose to breathe rather than react? How does that shift your experience?

# 15

# Eat dessert slowly, savoring the taste, texture, smell, and sight of your food

"Some of us, while looking at a piece of carrot, can see the whole
cosmos in it, can see the sunshine in it, can see the earth in it.
It has come from the whole cosmos for our nourishment.
You are capable of living in the present moment,
in the here and the now. It is simple, but you need some training
to just enjoy the piece of carrot. This is a miracle."
— *Thich Nhat Hanh*

$\mathcal{M}$ indful eating is a beautiful practice that helps us to cultivate presence. Eating is something that we do every day,
a few times a day, and it easily can become an act of unconsciousness.
We are busy at work, so we eat at our desks. We don't have time for
a healthy meal, so we buy something quickly made with little health
benefit for our bodies and eat it without awareness while driving to
our next destination. Bringing presence back to the act of eating is
one method of resting in ourselves. We can treat eating as a spiritual

practice. We literally are what we eat, as the food that we put into our bodies becomes our bones and tissues. And the way that we ingest our food is part of the assimilation process. We can make sitting and eating, without multitasking, the first part of the practice.

When we savor the taste, texture, sight, and smell of our food, we are interacting with the food through all of the senses. We have slowed down enough to really be present as we take in nourishment. The energy in the food is the same energy that flows through us. The yogic sages had a beautiful way of experiencing food—they saw the entire endeavor as divine. From the preparation to the ingestion to the digestion, they saw all parts of the meal and the person eating it as reflections of the ultimate reality.

These sages shared a food prayer that can be said prior to eating, to bring our minds into the experience of eating as a sacred action. When I learned this prayer, it touched my heart deeply and reminded me that there is nothing outside of the sacred, not even an action as run-of-the mill as eating. According to *Yoga International*, the English translation is:

"May I remember the truth: the food being offered is Brahman [ultimate reality], the individual offering the food is Brahman, and the process of offering itself is also Brahman. Therefore, I perform this offering with full awareness of Brahman alone. May the entire act of cooking, serving, and eating be transformed into sadhana [spiritual practice] leading us all toward Brahman, the highest goal of life. Through this offering may the universal consciousness that pervades and permeates the individual consciousness be worshipped and satisfied. Om, peace, peace, peace."

Whether you say this prayer or one of your own, the act of imbuing eating with a sacred pause helps you to savor and appreciate your food while you eat it. The act becomes its own prayer.

Paying attention to the taste of food puts us in the present. From an Ayurvedic perspective, there are six tastes: sweet, sour, salty, pungent, bitter, and astringent. All six tastes can be found in our food, and we can also think of life as having these six tastes. For many of us, it can be hard to find the sweet taste in life. We are rewarded for the saltiness of our speech, the spicy pungency of being goal driven, the drying astringency that being busy creates. The act of savoring or appreciating anything brings the sweet taste into our lives, and appreciating the experience of a delicious dessert is a double whammy of sweet taste (with everything in moderation, of course). The sweet taste builds our tissues, nurtures and nourishes us, and cools the fire of intensity. In Ayurveda, "sweet" does not mean "sugary." Foods like dates, which have no added sugar, fall into the category of sweet.

When home feels sweet and nurturing, we are more willing to want to rest there. Make a sweet treat for yourself, savor the experience of taking it into your body, and then pause. Know that the delight that you feel is always with you, and that the more you rest in that, a sense of delight permeates your being and your experience of life.

## Journal Contemplations

+ Does your diet include the sweet taste? What happens to your mind when you have just enough, and what's your experience of overdoing it?
+ Do you have enough sweet taste in your life? If not, what are some ways you could bring this in?
+ If the food prayer doesn't work for you, what is a method—from your own spiritual practice—that you could use to imbue eating with a sense of the sacred?

# 16

# Practice deep relaxation

"True silence is the rest of the mind; it is to the spirit
what sleep is to the body, nourishment and refreshment."
—William Penn

The art of relaxation is not one that we cultivate as a society. Here in the U.S., the value is placed on busyness, and though the desire is there to relax, many of us don't know how. It is easy to confuse relaxation with numbing out. Binge-watching your favorite television show, using alcohol to help slow the mind down, or overeating are some of the ways many of us try to relax during the busy workweek. While these activities are sure to slow us down, too much results in a sense of heaviness and stuckness.

Deep relaxation, on the other hand, helps us to cultivate light, clarity, and joy. Deep relaxation leaves us feeling rejuvenated, happier, and with a higher, grounded energy. It cultivates the healing hormones that neutralize the stress hormones which bombard our systems when we are constantly in a state of stress or busyness. Just like any other skill, the ability to deeply relax comes from practice. At first, we can feel really uncomfortable taking time out of our lives for relaxation. We may initially become jittery, restless, or anxious, as our nervous systems get used to slowing down. If we can breathe through this, there is another experience on the other side.

There are many different forms of deep relaxation, but the one I have found most beneficial is called Yoga Nidra, or yogic sleep. The best one I know of is recorded by my teacher, Rod Stryker, who describes the practice as "deep relaxation, with a slight trace of awareness." Yoga Nidra leaves you feeling as refreshed as a few hours of regular sleep. When I listen to Rod's short version (it's 27 minutes long), called *Relax into Greatness*, the stress of the day melts away, my mind feels more positive, and my body is refreshed. Other recordings made by teachers who have mastered this art have been made by Rolf Sovik and Richard Freeman, to name a few.

This deep-relaxation process brings balance to the body, breath, mind, and intellect. The systematic descent into consciousness and then back out resets us on all levels.

But when it comes to relaxation, for many people, the first question that will arise is, "How will I find the time?" A more useful question might be, "Is your own mental, emotional, and physical health worth setting aside time to relax? Can you invest a half-hour, one to three times a week, to reduce stress and cultivate lightness of being?"

When we give ourselves the gift of deep relaxation, the desire to come home to ourselves grows ever stronger. It's time for us to remove from our vocabulary any self-judgment regarding making time for ourselves. We need to let go of seeing healthy forms of relaxing as selfish, lazy, or a waste of time. We can retrain our minds to see deep relaxation as a trip to the gas station, filling ourselves up with the fuel of light and clarity that will serve us in all of our interactions out in the world.

During times of stress, I've noticed I can be resistant to setting aside time for things with no tangible end product. But as I've trained myself to take pauses and to slow down, I have seen that, at times, the most productive thing I can do for myself and everyone around me is to oil my body and lie down to do Yoga Nidra. The fullness that I feel when that practice is complete allows me to show up with more energy for everyone I'm in a relationship with, and for my work in the world.

Try this out for yourself. Find a recording that you like, lie down, and do the practice. After you finish Yoga Nidra, pause. Take a moment to appreciate tending to yourself in this way. Thank yourself for making time to come home.

## Journal Contemplations

- Are you willing to highly value feeling rested and centered as much as you value your achievements?
- Can you contextualize Yoga Nidra as an act of kindness toward yourself?
- What are the contents of any resistance to this practice, and how can you best release it?

# 17

# Spend time in the company of the wise, either in person, by reading a book, or by watching a video

"Satsanga, the company of the wise, is the way to attain the absolute good. It dispels the darkness of ignorance. The company of the wise yields the most desirable fruit."
— *Tripura Rahasya*

According to an ancient yogic text, *Tripura Rahasya*, one of the main afflictions of the mind is that we do things that steal our own joy. We allow ourselves to have thoughts and to engage in behaviors that lead to our forgetting what amazing beings we are. Our natural state is one of joy. But our ignorance of that state, and then the types of things we do as a result of that ignorance, keeps us from experiencing the natural state of joy that is our birthright.

One antidote to this mental suffering of stealing our own joy is being in the company of the wise (satsanga in Sanskrit). I've heard my spiritual teacher say that satsanga is the most effective antidote to ignoring the advice of your heart and acting against yourself and your own knowledge. When we spend time in the company of the wise, we place ourselves in environments that are spiritually supportive and lead us back to our true internal home.

The more time we spend in the company of the wise, the more we will begin to discern the difference between the behaviors and thought patterns that reinforce our joy and those that take us away from it. This joy is intrinsic and is not reliant on having something or not having it.

For those of us with easy access to our spiritual teachers, examples of satsanga would be attending a retreat, taking a yoga class with our favorite teacher, or having tea with that wise friend of ours in whose company we always remember the best of ourselves.

If you do not have a teacher just yet, or even friends in whose company you let your mind turn more toward the light, this is where spiritual texts come in. Pick up a copy of the *Upanishads*, *Gnostic Gospels*, the *Dhammapada*, or any other text from a tradition that inspires you and helps you to awaken to the depth of consciousness within you. Thankfully, because of the Internet, we can easily find videos of spiritual teachers giving talks or even spiritual podcasts, such as Krista Tippett's *On Being*. There are many ways to surround yourself with people who you feel are inspiring and who usher you into an experience of the deeper truths of living.

Part of my morning ritual is to start the day in the company of the wise by reading for a while from a spiritual text. I find that it helps me to start the day from a place of love and clarity, which is of immeasurable service to me as I move through the world for the rest of the day. You don't have to read for an hour. Some mornings, 15 minutes of reading is all that I can do. That sense of wisdom still seeps into my day. And on the days when my first postmeditation experience of the world is to check Facebook, I get sucked into a very different energy than when the first thing I do is to write or to read something with depth. I invite you to try out your own experiment.

Author Jim Rohn is credited with the quote, "You are the five people you spend the most of your time with." If that is true, why not make one of those people a wise friend or teacher who reminds you of your true nature? Let your time in the company of the wise reflect your inner light back to you. The cultivation of that inner light is a key component of building a desire to come home to ourselves.

After you spend some time in the company of the wise in whatever format you choose, pause. Breathe into the sense of stillness and luminosity that is present. Can you feel your own essence more deeply now? Take care to act from that place, in ways that support rather than steal your own joy.

## Journal Contemplations

+ What teachings help you to feel connected to your source?
+ Are you willing to give up one behavior that steals your joy?
+ What would be one behavior that you could add that would cultivate the company of the wise?

# 18

## Cultivate a new habit that supports your mind and body, and stick to it

"We are what we repeatedly do. Excellence, then,
is not an act, but a habit."
—*Aristotle*

One of the keys to excellence is knowing yourself, and a step on the pathway to Self-knowledge is personal practice. We can broaden the context of personal practice to include any activities that quiet your mind and bring you into a state of stillness, for in that stillness is the dawning of your irrevocable link to your true nature and the divine consciousness that is your source.

Sounds good, right? So why don't we do it? For many of us, delving into personal practice or stillness is something we do when we have extra time, or when we go on a retreat. That doesn't have to be the status quo, though. We can shift our lives to make personal practice a habit.

Habits are cultivated. Think about the first thing you do when you wake up. I must admit, there are days when I rub my eyes, lean over to kiss my husband, and then reach for my phone to check it for messages. It's a habit that arose quite innocently from leaving my phone on the nightstand next to the bed, checking it one morning, and then the next morning and the next and the next. While the morning smooch is welcome, I'm not so keen on the immediate screen time. I did not change that behavior until I formed a new habit: putting the phone on the dresser, out of arm's reach.

The good news is, we can cultivate supportive habits. We just need to make going to a class or doing a practice as much of a habit as the other things that we do as a matter of course without much fanfare. Many of us start to do so—we find that yoga class that we like, we put it on our schedule, and we start going twice a week. Then we get busy, and it falls off. Why? Sometimes it's because these practices require of us a willingness to allow ourselves to be changed. Since personal practice purifies our mind, it will burn off what no longer serves us. However, we are often attached to things that don't serve us, and there is a feeling of loss that goes with letting go of different behaviors, actions, and relationships through which we have defined ourselves. This resistance is often the hidden culprit behind our sudden inability to get to the class we were initially so excited about. To move through that resistance takes recommitting to cultivating that healing habit.

If you fall off, forgive yourself. And then add that yoga class, qi gong class, or meditation group back to your schedule, and commit to going twice a week. Treat it with the same level of inevitability as the fact that you will wake up and go to work. Notice the resistance when it arises—and go anyway. Building this habit is about committing to cultivating it and then recommitting when you find that you've moved away from it. Drop recrimination, which does not help you but only supports the inertia. Commit, recommit. We can make it that simple.

Know that whatever you feel like you are losing or giving up as you commit to this new habit is being released in service to your highest good. Your actions are making room for more light, more love, and more joy.

Imagine you've been living in one room your whole life. It is a beautiful room, and you've come to love it. It's comfortable, and it has everything you want. The room starts falling apart, and you can tell it's time to go. You mourn the loss of the room, and you're so upset about losing it that you don't notice the hole in the wall of the room opens up to an entire house. This house has plenty of space for you to grow and expand and step into the fullness that is your true nature. All you must do to have that experience is to let go of the room and step out into the rest of the house.

Your new habit, personal practice, is the purifier that shows you where the weak spots are in the room. Your willingness is the peephole from your old room to your new house. And your faith in the inner divine that you've been connecting with each time you practice—that faith supports you in stepping across the threshold into the new space, the more harmonious you.

Each time you engage in this new habit that is becoming a part of your life, pause. Be with yourself as you experience how the positive habit moves you toward an experience of your inner light. Relax into that light.

## Journal Contemplations

+ What do you notice about how you see yourself as you engage in your personal practice?
+ What new experiences arise from the discipline you're cultivating?
+ Can you be easy and kind with yourself both when you follow through on the commitment and when you don't?

# 19

# When you wake up in the morning, say aloud five things for which you are most grateful

"Gratitude turns what we have into enough, and more.
It turns denial into acceptance, chaos into order, confusion into
clarity . . . it makes sense of our past, brings peace for today,
and creates a vision for tomorrow."
— *Melody Beattie*

*T*he mental space that we cultivate in the morning often permeates the rest of our day. Think about the last time you started the day feeling late, rushing around like a maniac trying to get out of the house. Do you remember that rushed feeling following you through the rest of the day, as if you were being led around by your schedule? It's hard to rest in yourself when your relationship to time feels mired in scarcity.

You can have a huge, positive impact on the day by seeding your consciousness with uplifting energy. One easy way to do this is to begin the day with gratitude. When you wake up in the morning, say aloud five things for which you are most grateful. Starting the morning off by taking a few extra moments in bed to call in gratitude not only helps to slow down your mind, breath, and energy, but it also introduces a cooling and sweet energy to your mental field.

We can think of gratitude as plant food for the flower of abundance. The extent to which we can revel in gratitude for what we already have is the extent to which we open ourselves to receiving even more inner and outer wealth. As this practice becomes a part of your life, you'll experience the ebb and flow of ease with which you can touch the gratitude within. Some days you may feel it's a stretch, as if waking up this morning is the only thing you can find gratitude for. Other days, you'll wake up with gratitude flowing from your lips. Making this a practice over time fosters a sense of being less attached to gain and loss, and more centered in your ability to focus on the present, where you can see that you have what you need.

What is wealth? Is it money? Possessions? Stocks? Or is it love, family, and an inner sense of fulfillment? Is it all of the above? We all decide this for ourselves, but the practice of gratitude will teach you where you believe your treasure exists.

Drinking from the fountain of gratitude daily brings you closer to the light of your soul. The natural abundance, luminosity, and joy that pulses from the soul is more accessible to us when we find ways to feel gratitude for what we have. Taking nothing for granted is how we realize we are sitting on a pile of gold in life. There are sweet treasures in moments of connection and currents of expansion.

After your gratitude practice, pause. Breathe into the sense of expansiveness and gratitude for the divine energy in you that cocreates all of the inner and outer abundance that you have in your life.

# Journal Contemplations

* As you begin the gratitude practice, did you uncover any scarcity programming in your mind? If so, how can you let that go?
* What's going on in your life on the days when gratitude comes easily, and what's going on in your life on the days when you can barely think of five things?
* How do your relationships shift when you bring in this filter of looking for things for which to be grateful?

# 20

## Express yourself as if each day was your last

*"If I should die tomorrow, I will have no regrets.*
*I did what I wanted to do. You can't expect more from life."*
— *Bruce Lee*

$B$ecause as humans we are creative forces that are expressions of consciousness, the drive within us to express is strong. One of my favorite quotes about the power of expression is attributed to Jesus, in the *Gnostic Gospels*: "If you bring forth what is within you, what you bring forth will save you. If you do not bring forth what is within you, what you do not bring forth will destroy you." This drive to bring forth what is in us is operating from the moment our cells start to divide. That divine energy (Shakti), the spiritual power behind the constant multiplication and differentiation of cells that grows us from a zygote to a fully functioning human being, continues to burn bright in us throughout our whole lives. Sometimes we express it through *becoming*, the constant changes we make in our lives, and, sometimes, we express it through *being*, tapping into the stillness that lies at the center of us. Regardless of how it is showing up, that power to become and to be arises through us and wants to be expressed.

How do you prioritize expression in your life? We talk throughout the day, we do our work in the world, and, while these are forms of expression, in what ways are we approaching these as a vehicle to bring forth the magnitude that is in us? Are we expressing ourselves full out? Do we let our loved ones know, to the best of our ability, just how much we love them? When we notice something we appreciate about another, do we take the time to share it? When we go to work, do we see the way we complete our actions as a form of expressing our purpose?

Life is not a given. We have no idea how long or in what form it will last. Author and palliative-care nurse Bonnie Ware illustrates this point in her book *The Top Five Regrets of the Dying: A Life Transformed by the Dearly Departing*. Dying patients shared with her their top five regrets:

+ "I wish I'd had the courage to live a life true to myself, not the life others expected of me.
+ I wish I hadn't worked so hard.
+ I wish I'd had the courage to express my feelings.
+ I wish I had stayed in touch with my friends.
+ I wish that I had let myself be happier."

Each of these regrets relates in part to how or what we choose to express or not express, and the noticing and breaking down of barriers to expression. Don't wait until the end of life to let that consciousness that wants to be expressed through you have its say. It's not only death that offers this reflective pause to us. I have found that each time I experienced a deep loss or an intense life shift, there's a moment of recollection, of noticing how I stopped paying attention to my inner compass. The inner compass intuits the balance of expression and experiencing, being and becoming, connecting outward and drawing inward.

The great thing about being human is that each moment, each day, is an opportunity to start over. So, let's start today. All throughout your day, pay attention to your signals that expression is bubbling forth. Honor those signals in whatever way meets that energy. And at the end of your day, pause, and breathe. Notice, is there anything in you that wants to be expressed that was not during this day? Go ahead and let that happen naturally. This might look like journaling, painting, talking to your beloved, or any form the life force in you wants to take. Breathe into the sense of freedom and expansiveness that comes from feeling fully expressed.

Giving ourselves permission to move through the world in this way has a positive ripple effect on the people around us. When we give that power to become and to be its fullest expression, we honor ourselves, and we honor the source from which we came. That deep sense of honoring is a gateway to feeling at home in ourselves, wherever we are. When we rest our heads at night and, based on our actions, we feel complete with each interaction, each expression, each choice we made through the day—we are building a foundation of meeting life on life's terms.

## Journal Contemplations

+ As you explored this suggestion, did unanswered desires to paint, dance, write, or create arise?
+ What is one element of your way of being that feels uniquely yours?
+ How do you soften your inner critic when you express in a way that feels new to you?

# 21

# Learn about your divine nature

"For he who has not known himself has known nothing,
but he who has known himself has at the same time already
achieved knowledge about the depth of the all."
— *The Book of Thomas the Contender,* Gnostic Gospels

*T*here are many paths to getting to know your deepest Self, and one of the best ways I know of is meditation. My second-favorite method is to spend time in Nature, as it calms the nervous system and has an internalizing impact on the mind. After years of leading participants through meditation practices while out in Nature, I have witnessed time and time again how these amazing beings have been excited and humbled by what they experienced when they rested in their own hearts.

There are books we can read that point us to our innate divinity. But the way to acquire knowledge and wisdom is through direct experience. Just like with anything we are trying to learn, we have to make time to practice. It's the same with wanting to learn our most essential, divine nature. We need to make time every day to get to know our deepest Self.

To that end, I'd like to share a meditation that came into my mind in the wee hours of the morning. It is likely a mixture of a number of different meditations I've done with my teachers over the years. I find it helpful to do this meditation in moments when I feel disconnected from a sense of well-being, and it has served to help me feel connected again. I use the word "Divine" in it, which can mean whatever makes you feel a sense of interconnectedness. Some call it Spirit, Nature, Oneness, Energy, Source, or Goodness. Please relate to this vastness in any way that lets you truly feel connected to that energy in you.

You can practice this meditation in an open-ended way, or you can set a timer so that it is for a specific amount of time. Choose whichever method helps you to be most present with the practice.

To practice the Divine Breath Meditation, please find a place in Nature. From your back yard to a public park, find a place where you can get down on the ground and feel your connection to the earth.

Come to a comfortable cross-legged seat with your head, neck, and trunk in a straight line over your hips. With a relaxed abdomen, begin to breathe into your belly. Take a few diaphragmatic breaths, as you scan your body and invite all of the muscle groups to relax.

Once this breath feels comfortable and is smooth and unrushed, start to shape your breath so that your inhalation and exhalation are even. Try in for a count of four and out for four if you are new to this way of breathing.

When this breath begins to feel easy, invite into your heart a sense of well-being or calm. You can think of a person or place or animal that invokes this in you.

As you breathe in, sense that you are breathing in divinity, permeating all of the spaces in your body. As you breathe out, sense your exhale being breathed in by divinity.

Stay with this feeling. With each in-breath, you draw in divinity. With each out-breath you take, the divine breathes you in. If emotion arises, let it flow while bringing your attention back to the meditation.

Every breath reinforces this innate connection between you and the divine. The divine is in you, and you are in the divine. There is no separation. There is only connection.

After you complete the meditation, pause. What has shifted for you? Notice your body. Notice your breath. Notice your mind. Feel the increased sense of presence and embodiment that comes with meditation.

## Journal Contemplations

+ As we practice this meditation, our limiting beliefs may come up, and our mind may present all the ways we judge ourselves not to be divine. If this happened for you, please journal what those limiting beliefs were, and then, afterward, write down, "Still divine."
+ How did being in Nature support your ability to come back to the meditation when your mind began to wander?
+ How does learning about your divine nature support your sense of aliveness and purpose?

# 22

## Forgive yourself for that one thing that you use to beat yourself up

*"The weak can never forgive.*
*Forgiveness is the attribute of the strong."*
*— Mahatma Gandhi*

W e all have it—that one thing that we use to beat ourselves up. You know the one. It is very reliable. Every time life gets good, your inner critic trots that one out as if to say, "Oh, yeah? What about *this?*"

Are you ready to stop doing that to yourself? Forgiveness is a miracle. Anger or pain or judgment is a state of contraction, one in which the energy and communication toward another person, and toward our experience of our own divine nature, feels cut off. Forgiveness is the medicine that lets us experience again how that energy and communication is always flowing. That energy is how we communicate with the divine, so when we hold on to grudges against ourselves, we are saying to that divine energy, "I'm separate from you. I don't think you permeate all existence because you are not in this place."

Everything we experience in life begins in our internal landscape. Our lives arise from the conditions of our mind. When we start experiencing lots of turmoil in relationships, we must be experiencing lots of turmoil in our relationship with ourselves. The deep sense of separation and aloneness that we feel when we are on the outs with someone we love is the same separation and aloneness we feel when we shut off the connection between ourselves and the inner divine. The same healing balm of forgiveness that we use with others works internally, too.

For you, what is the decision, experience, or moment that is the pin that you use to keep poking yourself, all the while saying, "Ouch"? For me, many years ago, it was getting a divorce. When I spoke of it, I would use the phrase "my divorce," which signals how much I was identified with it. To me it was the consummate failure, the proof that I am fundamentally flawed and can't have sustainable relationships. The stain of judgment that I felt each time I checked the box "divorced" felt like a mark on my forehead that everyone could see and judge. One day I was talking to a friend, and she was having a bad day. I asked what was going on, and she said it was the anniversary of when she and her ex-husband had gotten married. I hugged her and offered her comfort. Later, when I got home, I marveled at how differently I treated myself. I didn't judge her for being divorced, because, of course, I understood that sometimes marriages do not last, for a variety of reasons. But here I was, not affording myself the same benefit of the doubt, and instead holding it over my head every chance I got. *If you wouldn't treat a dear friend that way, why would you treat yourself that way?* I asked internally. That was the beginning of the process of forgiveness, for me, from me.

What negative story are you running that is so reliable that, no matter how much growth and expansion you achieve, it is so familiar to you that you always return to it? Let that one arise in your consciousness. Feel as though you can see it, the size of it, the shape of it, the texture of it. Take a few breaths into your heart space, and feel as though a healing, rose light arises there. See that rose light completely bathing your pain in the light of forgiveness. Internally say to yourself, *I forgive myself for this.* Ask the divine within you to forgive you. And know that since that divine within you sees you as whole and complete and lacking nothing, She knows that there is nothing to forgive. You were never separate, and there is nothing you could do that would break your connection to the love and light that is within you. Your mind can only obscure your ability to feel it. Pause now, resting in the illumination of wholeness.

If you are in a bright and beautiful room, but you put a room-darkening blanket over your head, does that mean the light went off? Of course not. Your lack of awareness of it doesn't mean it isn't there. Forgiveness is the means by which you take the blanket off of your head. And as you forgive yourself, you remember to see the light in others as well.

In yoga, we talk a lot about ahimsa, the principle of nonharming. Many people feel that, by not eating meat, they are really living into this principle. You can be as lacto-ovo, vegan, no oil as you want to be, but if you are beating yourself up regularly, that is the mental equivalent of eating all of the prime rib, plus a milkshake. Ahimsa starts internally.

Let forgiveness connect you back to your source. Let forgiveness bring you home to yourself.

# Journal Contemplations

- Do you have a belief that forgiving yourself or someone else means giving up something? Are you willing to let that go?
- What self-harming habits do you have, and can you create a plan to release these systematically over the next few months?
- As you practice forgiving yourself with more ease, do you notice any shifts in how much energy is available to you?

# 23

## Read yourself
## a Hafiz poem aloud

"Sing
Because this is a food
Our starving world
Needs.
Laugh
Because that is the purest
Sound."
— *Hafiz*

*H*afiz was a Persian poet and mystic who wrote about the Divine as his Beloved. His poems touch on themes of joy and faith, and constantly affirm the love between ourselves and the divine within. His poetry is a reminder of the sacred that is found in every action, every experience, every breath, and also a reminder that we can hold all experience lightly. The humor he infuses into his poetry is like a breath of fresh air.

We read to children often, but how often do you read to yourself? What I love about reading aloud to yourself is that it evokes a sweet sense as you bask in the gift of your own exquisite attention. How beautiful to be able to turn our gaze both to the divine in us and to our individual soul, and all with the energy of play.

I like to read Hafiz in the morning as a way of infusing the day with a playful connection to my beloved in the form of the divine. Reading aloud also gives you a chance to hear the beauty of a heartfelt prayer spoken from your own lips. After you read a poem, pause. Revel in the honey of devotional love.

My mornings used to be infused with a sense of rushing to get a headstart on what was most likely going to be a very busy day. It is hard to feel connected to yourself, let alone connected to the source of all life, when life is rushed, and you feel like you barely have time to sit down and breathe. I found that reading aloud was so sensual. The vibration of the words landed me back in myself. Reading about a love so deep, pure, and all-encompassing opened me up to my own longing for that experience. By reading Hafiz's experience, I went there. The physical sensation of taking in his art was so deeply pleasurable. There is a gift in turning toward what feels enjoyable and enlivening throughout the day. It's like a refresher for your body, mind, and spirit.

Taking a pause to invite the divine into our hearts sets an internal sense of stillness that we can return to throughout the day. Just like physical-muscle memory, when we make it a practice to invite the divine into our hearts, we have that mental-muscle memory and can drop into this space when we choose to throughout the day. The playful energy of Hafiz reminds us that we don't have to approach the divine with a heavy and serious energy. If She is in everything, then She is in play as well. When we open up to the playful part of ourselves, we open up to the divine within.

## Journal Contemplations

- Is devotion new for you? What is your relationship to spiritual love?
- How is play a gateway to expansion in your life?
- In what ways does the all-encompassing flavor of love for the divine make you feel more connected?

# 24

## Draw or paint the way that you feel

"The purpose of art is washing the dust of daily life off our souls."
— *Pablo Picasso*

From an Ayurvedic perspective, emotions need to be digested, just like food. The term for the fire of digestion is called agni. This agni has a gastric form that has the power to digest our food and a mental form that has the power to digest our emotions.

We live in a world where emotions have a negative connotation. People are ridiculed for being emotional, those who express their feelings freely are seen as irrational, and traditional gender roles narrow the scope for feeling and expressing emotion.

If we think of emotion as material that is a biochemical response that needs to be digested, we can see how the constant suppression of emotion could, at a very chemical level, have a long-term unhealthy impact on the body. Imagine eating heavy (sad), salty (angry), spicy (fear) food all day long without being able to digest it. After a while, you'd vomit. It's no wonder that people are scared to feel their feelings. There is so much undigested material that, when we do let ourselves feel, the buildup is such that the emotions may feel overwhelming. A key to coming home to yourself is to digest emotions each day rather than waiting until the buildup overwhelms you.

The digestion process starts with presence. The act of observation without needing to change anything is the digestion. Art can be a great ally at this stage. Drawing or painting is a great way to digest your feelings.

The huge waves of loss that crashed through me after a major life transition, coupled by the ungrounding sense of not knowing what the future held in terms of love and family, felt almost like drowning. And the pain was such that I didn't feel I had access to my usual outlet of words. I turned to pastels. I had no training or familiarity with pastels, so the newness of that medium matched how newly I was experiencing myself and my surroundings. The feelings I couldn't put into words just flowed out on to the canvas, and suddenly, I had a way to be with my experience more deeply.

In the process of creating art, you first turn your awareness inward. What emotions can you get in touch with, and once you make contact, how does that move you to connect with your canvas or paper? After you've let the emotion move through you, out onto the paper, pause. Take a breath or two, and notice the joy of having transformed an emotion into an act of expression.

The creative principle is within all of us. Giving ourselves the freedom to draw or paint or use any medium to express ourselves is freeing in a huge way. We clear out the space that undigested emotion clogs up, leaving us with more room for joy, love, and creativity. We don't have to "know how." Your hand knows how to express what's inside of you.

It's important not to judge or evaluate the expression. It's bringing something inside of you out into the world of form, and that is enough. You are enough. These forms of expression are the breadcrumbs back to aspects of ourselves we have long forgotten.

## Journal Contemplations

+ When you bring your awareness to an emotion, can you feel the difference between your nonjudgmental awareness and self-judgment?
+ What medium matches the emotion you're wanting to digest and express?
+ What conditions promote an experience of drawing or painting that feels meditative rather than like a task to check off?

# 25

# Lie on your back with your legs up the wall for 10 minutes, breathing deeply and abdominally

"Viparita Karani: Place the head on the ground and the feet up into the sky, for a second only the first day, and increase this time daily. After six months, the wrinkles and grey hair are not seen. He who practices it daily, even for two hours, conquers death."
—*Hatha Yoga Pradipika*

Initiating the relaxation response is a key method for coming home to yourself. Making time for deep relaxation helps to reduce anxiety and promote a sense of well-being. The yoga posture called "legs up the wall pose" (Viparita Karani) is one such pause that we can initiate at the end of the day (or any time we need it, for that matter).

Many of us are moving through the world with taxed adrenals. Our bodies are responding to the busyness of life by constantly releasing stress hormones. It's hard to turn inward when you have natural chemicals coursing through your veins that are stimulating and over time result in feelings of anxiety and irritation. The fight-or-flight portion of our nervous systems can tend to be overworked.

Taking 10 minutes for yourself to lie down on your back with your legs up the wall while breathing into your belly fully and deeply can help you begin to activate your parasympathetic nervous system. This part of the nervous system, which allows us to rest and digest (not only our food but also all the information and experiences that we collect), gets activated and initiates the release of hormones that balance the overabundance of stress hormones. If your mind isn't able to quiet when it's time to go to sleep, this posture can help with that insomnia.

The results of 10 minutes in this pose are profound. Over time and with continued practice, the pose has helped shift my entire outlook from feeling jittery, tired, and overwhelmed to feeling grounded and internalized. I become present and let go of what is bothering me long enough that I can see the issue from a different perspective. Of course, yoga postures are not panaceas or fast-acting cures. It's the practice of getting into legs up the wall pose over and over again that trains my body and mind to know it's an opportunity to relax.

Most importantly, the combination of belly breathing and lying down and allowing ourselves to be supported both by the wall against our legs and the earth against our back reminds us of the support that is always there. We can lift ourselves up by laying down—by carving out space for breath and awareness, and giving ourselves the gift of our presence. And when we relax into the natural support of the earth under us and the structures around us, we are relaxing into grace. We are giving the reactive brain a break and moving into the part of the brain that is about choosing and creating.

The force that brought you into this world has not forgotten you, but it is hard to feel that when we are muscling through life. Legs up the wall pose is an opportunity to reestablish our connection with ourselves and also have the felt experience of that larger and eternal support of the universe.

## Journal Contemplations

- What other activities do you do that allow you to rest and digest?
- Do you notice you feel more jittery when you first lie down? If so, how does deepening your diaphagmatic breathing shift your experience?
- Is any part of you resistant to relaxing, because you're used to fueling your drive with adrenaline? Are you open to a different fuel for your endeavors?

# 26

# Reach out to a dear friend, and share the qualities you most appreciate about them

"Appreciation is a wonderful thing.
It makes what is excellent in others belong to us as well."
—*Voltaire*

Community is valued in all wisdom traditions. Christians enjoy fellowship with other members of the church. Buddhists take refuge in the spiritual community (sangha). Ayurveda teaches that one of the top ways to build natural vigor and immunity (ojas) is through connecting with your sangha. Our ancestors knew it took a village to raise a child, and we are all children of the Divine. No matter where we are in life, there are likely people who have helped us to get there through their love, support, and presence.

We offer a beautiful gift when we share appreciations for someone we love. A side benefit is that the gift of appreciation is a boomerang, so when you share an appreciation with another, you are appreciating those same qualities in yourself. Your ability to bear witness to the good in another opens a channel for you to experience your own innate goodness. Of course, we wouldn't offer our appreciation to others *because* of the boomerang effect. We appreciate them because when love happens, we want to call it out, we want to celebrate it, we want to shine a light on it, because we don't take it for granted.

Who is the person you call when there's a big event in your life? Who is the dear friend that you turn to when surfing the waves of your highest highs and your lowest lows?

Bring that person into your awareness. Breathe into the image that comes into your mind and the accompanying love you feel for them. Once you have called in this friend, feel into what you appreciate about them the most. Notice the particular flavor of your appreciation for this dear friend, observing the unique way in which they are a friend to you.

According to *Love 2.0* by Barbara Fredrickson, a study found that mind-training related to building positivity and connection helped to increase vagal tone, which directly impacts a person's health. When we train our minds to focus on love, we build our ability to connect with others. Fredrickson found, through her research on loving-kindness meditation, that "those who experienced the most frequent positivity resonance in connection with others showed the biggest increases in vagal tone. Love literally made people healthier."

While appreciating your dear ones is not the same as a formal loving-kindness meditation practice, I have found great joy in "leading with appreciation," a technique taught by Kathlyn Hendricks. The act of mentally appreciating someone before speaking with them creates a context of connection in which the interaction is primed by an underlying tone of positivity and love.

Extend this context to your friend. Share your appreciation for them in a personal way, perhaps through a phone call, writing a letter or an email, texting, or even a video call. Share three qualities that you really appreciate. Feel the openness of your heart that comes from recognizing the divinity in another and letting Her know She is seen. Breathe into that bridge that opens from your heart to your friend's.

We are all connected. When we give love, we are also receiving love. Part of coming home to yourself is not only learning to hold your own hand but taking time to appreciate those in your life who have held your hand, perhaps even when you forgot to hold your own.

## Journal Contemplations

+ What do you notice about turning an appreciative gaze toward your friend?
+ What body sensations accompany your sharing of appreciations?
+ If resistance comes up, can you notice its presence and recommit to the practice?

# 27

# Cook yourself
# a nourishing meal

"Cooking is at once child's play and adult joy.
And cooking done with care is an act of love."
—*Craig Claiborne*

*W*hen it comes to cooking, many of my clients have fallen into the "cooking relaxes me" camp, the "I do it because I have to" camp, or the "eating out most nights" camp. Personally, I cook out of necessity, as it isn't something I turn to for either fun or relaxation. I don't feel particularly skilled at it, and my inner perfectionist thinks there's too much room for error. But as my Ayurvedic studies deepened, I started to want to eat according to the foods that most kept me in balance and realized it's hard to eat in a way that feels healthy and enlivening when I'm eating out too often. Feeding yourself is nourishing. It's a form of self-love. Outsourcing that to any number of restaurants, no matter how amazing, felt, to me, like I was skipping over an opportunity for nurturing.

Recently, I realized it was time to release the old "I can't stand cooking because I'm not good at it" story and write a new one. The best part about writing a new story is that you get to make every aspect of it your own. You can choose to do it the way you want to rather than how you were taught or what you've done in the past. If you've struggled with cooking at home, ask yourself, "How could it be different this time?"

As a lover of chanting, it occurred to me that, as I was preparing the food, I could chant the *Annapurna Stotram* over the meal. This Vedic chant to the Divine Mother in the form of food is so beautiful that I have never chanted it without some tears forming in my eyes. The energy of the mantra is so sweet and loving. Perhaps you have a chant or a song you could sing that you feel would add some extra nurturing into the food.

In addition to inviting in the spiritual component of cooking and eating, I also recommend keeping it as fun as possible. For me, that means adding some movement. I highly recommend hip shaking while chopping vegetables. Permission to make a mistake is important, too. For many of us who aren't enamored of cooking, part of that has to do with having a very loud inner perfectionist. If that voice arises, take a deep breath, and remember to be your own best friend rather than your own worst critic. Give yourself permission to find your way, rather than adhere to some idea of what a good cook looks like. Trust that attention to your breath, and awareness and release of any inner criticism can help you to soften.

Ayurveda teaches that a balanced meal has all six tastes: sweet, salty, sour, pungent, bitter, and astringent. Sweet foods include sweet potatoes and basmati rice (take care not to confuse "sweet" with "sugary"). Salty foods include seaweed or cottage cheese. Sour foods include yogurt or lemons. Pungent foods include garlic or onions. Bitter foods include coffee and dark leafy greens. Astringent foods include beans or tea. These are just a few examples of six taste foods that you might already have in your house. As you craft your meal, giving attention to these six tastes will create even more balance and nourishment as a result.

After you're done eating, pause. Breathe in appreciation for the nourishment of the food, the earth that grew the food, the farmers who harvested it, and yourself for cooking it. Enjoy the feeling of having nurtured yourself and having made the experience fun.

## Journal Contemplations

- In your journey of cooking yourself a meal, what were you doing when you found it hard to treat yourself with kindness? Can you bring light to those places?
- Whether you're a new cook or a seasoned one, can you approach the kitchen with curiosity and a beginner's mind?
- Are there any shifts you can make to your schedule to have some spaciousness around the act of cooking?

# 28

# Practice loving-kindness meditation

"To reteach a thing its loveliness is the nature of metta.
Through loving kindness, everyone and everything
can flower again from within."
—*Sharon Salzberg*

Years ago, my spiritual teacher taught me that energy follows thought. It's essentially a loop, because, as you think about something, your energy starts to collect there, and, as your energy collects, your mind is drawn to that place as well. Can you see that operating in your own life? When you spend a lot of time ruminating or thinking about what could go wrong, do you find that the more you think about it and the more energy you expend toward defending against it, it almost becomes a self-fulfilling prophecy? This same loop happens when we turn our mind toward the positive. The Buddhist practice of loving kindness (metta) is a beautiful way to collect our energy and awareness on the field of love.

Center yourself by taking a few deep diaphragmatic breaths. Once you feel present, soften and allow a sense of love to wash over you. From that energy of love, you first turn the act of loving kindness toward yourself.

+ May I be happy.
+ May I be healthy.
+ May I feel safe.
+ May I live with ease.

Pause between each one, making sure that your own wish for yourself really lands on you and that you receive it. Breathe deeply, experiencing each line of the meditation before you move on to the next one. Sometimes resistance arises, and if that occurs, observe it, soften, and open again to that pervasive energy of love that is always around us. Many of us have no problem turning that love stream outward, and yet it can be hard sometimes to flow that love toward ourselves.

Metta is a practice that brings us into a state of loving kindness. In my experience, the result is a softening of the heart and an expansion of the energy there. I feel a relaxing of the thought patterns that sometimes keep me from being kind and supportive to myself and grounding to those I care about.

After we fill our own cups, the next step in metta practice is to send it to loved ones, neutral people, people whom we find challenging, and all beings. By learning to include ourselves and everyone we know in this loving-kindness practice, we are cultivating compassion, which is the active principle of love.

Love is the underlying intelligence that pulses through everything. It is all too easy to forget who we really are, to identify so much with what we have and what we do, that we forget we are consciousness *experiencing* these states of being and that we are not defined by the states we experience.

Metta practice brings us home to ourselves in that we immerse our minds and hearts in that love from which we came, the love that never left, and that is available to us always.

## Journal Contemplations

+ When you practice metta, do you feel the strength of loving kindness, or do you have an experience of it as a liability?
+ Can you try this practice next time you're in a line at the store or another public place? How does that shift your experience?
+ What are the body sensations of loving kindness?

# 29

# Write a love letter to the beloved inside of you

"Find the love you seek, by first finding the love within yourself.
Learn to rest in that place within you that is your true home."
—*Sri Sri Ravi Shankar*

One way to come home to yourself is to write a love letter to the beloved inside of you. Having this love expressed on paper gives you the ability to touch that place at a later date, when you've forgotten. A free-form, stream-of-consciousness love letter written from that place of deep connection to your own vastness can be a touchstone in those moments when you feel disconnected from yourself and your source.

How does your love for the divinity in you want to be expressed? Here is a letter that I wrote to myself at a time when I noticed I was so identified with my mistakes that I was forgetting to relate to myself as awesomely, beautifully human.

*I'm writing to remind you of your inner wealth. We all forget sometimes. I forgive you for forgetting, and I forgive you for the decisions you've made because you don't remember. I just want to remind you. You are vast consciousness in human form.*

*Your body is amazing. Look at all of the things it can do. You have hands to reach for what you want. You have feet to take you to wherever you need to go. You have a voice that allows you to express your ideas and feelings. You have one half of the equipment it takes to make another human being. And your body knows how to separate what it needs from everything that you've taken in, so it can eliminate the rest. So much of what your amazing vessel can do is automatic. And that's just at the most basic level. You can train it to do the most amazing things, like yoga, singing, dancing, painting, and playing. Your body is capable of countless experiences.*

*You are gifted with the ability to see, hear, touch, taste, and smell. Through you, consciousness gets to have an embodied experience. Your mind stores your myriad feelings, thoughts, experiences, and habits so effortlessly it makes IBM's Watson computer look like an abacus. It holds your sense of uniqueness, your you-ness, your ability to be ready and willing to show up as only you can. Your mind is endowed with clarity and inner knowing. The sages saw that each of our souls has four desires: the desire to fulfill our unique purpose for being here, the desire for the means to fulfill our purpose, the desire to experience love and beauty as we fulfill our purpose, and the desire to experience peace and freedom. Through the deepest part of your intellect, you can hear the desires of your individual soul, the part of you that is eternal.*

*Breathe that in. You are the light of consciousness endowing a physical form. You are here, quite literally, on a mission of fulfillment and freedom. Honor your body. Give it movement. Give it deep breath. Let yourself relax deeply. Give your body love. Stop saying bad things about it. Stop comparing* it to other bodies. Give it moments of stillness. Put food into it that keeps it running optimally. Thank your body for serving you and housing your consciousness and letting you move ever closer to the desires of your soul. Know that your body and mind are deeply connected and work together. Accept them both as they are, and from that place of acceptance, make choices that honor your wholeness. Be willing to let go of seeing yourself as anything other than amazing.

Life is beautiful. It is a gift. I know things happen in your life that make you see it differently. And yet even in the midst of whatever that hardship is, notice that you are breathing. Let your breath, the animator of your body, the inhale and the exhale, let that be a reminder to you of the magic of being alive. Feel your breath infusing your body and mind with energy as divinity flows into you and out of you with each breath cycle. Allow that divinity in you to help you remember your full capability. Reclaim your essence.

As you craft your own letter, feel free to take from this whatever works for you. Allow yourself to start from where you are, loving what you can, in a way that feels real to you. When you finish, pause, breathe, and notice how you feel having just shined your love toward yourself in a very practical way.

## Journal Contemplations

- What aspects of yourself were easy for you to write a love letter to, and what aspects were challenging to embrace?
- Think of a time when you wrote a love letter to someone. What's your experience of shining that same adoration toward yourself?
- Do you feel you are deserving of your own loving expression in this way?

# 30

## Give to someone

"To give and to receive are one in truth."
—*A Course in Miracles*

We feel good when we give. We feel good when we share the abundance that we enjoy. Everyone wins, whether it's the charitable organization you're donating to, the people it serves, and your own heart. I have found that giving money and time reminds me of my inherent state of fullness and shakes loose any beliefs about scarcity. There is always enough. It doesn't have to be a huge amount; it can be whatever you desire to gift so that someone else who is in need receives your gift and has the felt sense that they are supported by the community and by life itself.

Perhaps you've had the experience of someone giving you just what you needed at just the right time. When we receive such a gift, we're reminded that we are always supported and cared for as well. It's a great feeling to be able to do that for someone else. In this context of giving, it could be whatever need wants to be filled. Whether it's giving of our attention or time, or giving money or a meal, perhaps even lending our skills to someone in need, when we give, we experience how deep our inner well runs.

Magically, as we give, we receive as well. Giving is an inherent recognition and appreciation for the fact that you have enough to share. This is why it can be so healing to give even when your mind is mired in a sense of scarcity, because it reminds you of your inherent fullness. Even when your deepest scarcity stories are running, you can still give love.

Giving is one of the best ways I know of to move out of a contracted state. Giving creates a felt sense of inner spaciousness. Just like with anything else, though, it can be a poison as well as a medicine. When we aren't taking care of ourselves, and we are trying to take care of everyone else, that's not the type of giving that supports expansion. True giving comes from a place of recognizing that both the receiver and the giver are whole and complete, and it is that wholeness and completeness that allows the giving to reinforce an inner sense of abundance in both parties. The inherent and fundamental equality of the two people, regardless of the circumstances they find themselves in, is what keeps the giving and receiving at the level of spirit rather than ego.

Giving brings you home to yourself, because you remember that you have enough and that you are enough. You remember your own wholeness, and it is that remembrance that means you're home. After you find a way to give to someone, pause. Be with the fullness of your heart in that moment.

## Journal Contemplations

* What are your go-to scarcity stories, and where did you learn them?
* When you give from a place of wholeness for everyone involved, how does that shift your experience?
* How does giving put you in touch with your inner wealth?

# 31

# Put on your favorite song,
# and sing your heart out

"The only thing better than singing is more singing."
—*Ella Fitzgerald*

I distinctly remember driving down the street one day, blasting Adele, singing along like her very own personal backup singer. As my voice stretched and expanded (in a humorously failed but very enjoyable effort to meet hers), I had the sensation of shackles being taken off of something that had long wanted to roam free. I remember asking myself, "When did you stop singing?" It begged a number of other questions—"When did you start stifling the fullness of your expression in the interest of being 'normal'?" "When did leading with your intellect take a front seat over being authentic?" "When did avoiding feeling judged become more important than just being yourself and doing your work in the world?" "When did holding back become a way of life?"

It is a brave and scary thing to live full out. Often we are bombarded with images that tell us to fit in rather than those that support authenticity. Even in so-called spiritual communities, there is pressure to conform. "Oh you aren't practicing this form of yoga or that form of meditation, or studying with this teacher or doing this practice?" Fail! These forms of spiritual materialism actually take us further away from the teachings rather than toward a direct experience of them.

We internalize these limiting views, and rather than feeling shut down only by the world, we start to do it to ourselves. We start saying, "I can't (sing, dance, write, paint, take a class, or find new interests)." Often, after digging into that a bit, it's more that "We won't," because we judge our own expression as being of poor quality, or we compare ourselves to someone else and come up short. What does life look like when we stop doing that to ourselves? There's only one way to find out.

I have had a number of clients who, when they start learning about body awareness, share that when they go to express, they have a lump in their throat. As we investigate that lump, there can be a lifetime of unspoken words, uncried tears, and pent-up expression that is forming that lump. Whatever form you choose for releasing your authentic expression, do it in a way that honors you.

Let your inner wild horse of expression run free, released from the shackles of self-judgment or caring what others may think. Watch how that freedom brings you back to your center, that place in you that is pure being, pure love, pure joy. The exhilaration of showing up for yourself in this way is magical. But we aren't chasing a high—rather, we are taking this action so that our full expression becomes a matter of course rather than a periodic occurrence.

Give yourself a three-minute dip into the experience of unbridled expression by putting on your favorite song and singing your heart out. Afterward, pause. Breathe. Be fully with the experience of your own expression. Rest in yourself, knowing that this expression is a manifestation of the consciousness that moves through everything.

## Journal Contemplations

+ How is the fullness of your expression, in all its beautiful notes and discordant ones, of service to everyone around you?
+ Where are the places where you're trying to fit in, and what does moving toward authenticity look like for you?
+ What price do you pay for suffocating your inner expression?

# 32

# Gaze at a candle until your eyes tear and you see the flame in your mind's eye, and then meditate on that flame

"Trataka eradicates all eye diseases, fatigue, and sloth, and closes the doorway creating these problems."
—*Hatha Yoga Pradipika*

*F*ire is mesmerizing. Whether it's a campfire out in the woods or a fire in a fireplace, at some point in your life, you have likely been entranced by the dancing of the flame. Fire warms us, it nurtures us, cooks our food, and lights our way. Mentally we cultivate the fire of our intelligence and discernment. Physically, we each have our own portion of this divine flame, in the form of our digestive fire, and the strength of this inner fire directly correlates to our health and our ability to shine in the world. One way to stoke this fire, as well as to cleanse and nurture the eyes, is to practice candle gazing. This practice, called trataka, is a method that can also help us to enter into meditation.

To practice candle gazing, come into a comfortable seated position, in a dark room, on a blanket or cushion, so your hips are slightly higher than your knees. Sit up straight, yet relaxed, so your head, neck, and trunk are in a straight line over your hips. Take a few deep breaths, regulating any rough or rushed portions of your breath cycle.

Once you feel relaxed and present, with a smooth breath, place a lit candle at eye level, and gaze at a point in the center of the candle. Keep your awareness at the point, without blinking, as long as possible, until your eyes begin to tear. Once the eyes are tearing, allow the eyes to close, and you'll notice that you likely see the imprint of the flame even with closed eyes. If not, open your eyes, and gaze more. Once you do see the flame with closed eyes, let that be the point of your focus for meditation. As thoughts arise, notice them, but don't get involved. Bring the awareness back to the mental imprint of the flame.

After you practice candle gazing, pause. Take a few breaths. Create some space after the practice—space for you to just rest in being. When we pause the momentum of our lives and devote some of our time to being with this fire, we turn back toward our source. Touching that external fire brings us back into contact with the fire within. This fire calls us back home, bringing us into the experience of resting fully in ourselves, feeling whole and complete.

Trataka is not necessarily easy, but when I first started practicing meditation, I found that it was more accessible to me than watching the breath, or even mantra meditation. Having an external focus that then moved to an internal focus really worked for my busy mind. If you feel that meditation isn't for you, give this a try, as you might find it calms your mind and you're able to focus much better than with more subtle points of focus, like the breath.

According to the yogic sages, fire is the divine. Agni, or fire, is the first word of the Vedas, which are the Indian texts that codify spiritual wisdom. Trataka stokes our agni and helps us begin to develop a relationship with divinity in the form of fire. That fire is light and life. That fire is you.

## Journal Contemplations

+ What's your relationship to your inner fire?
+ Start slow by adding this practice to your day for five minutes. How is your experience later in the day impacted? When you feel ready, increase the time by a few minutes.
+ Do you have a sense for what activities brighten your fire and what activities dull it?

# 33

# Notice those places inside that hurt, and bring some love there

"The wound is the place where the Light enters you."
—*Rumi*

*W*e all have the power to bring healing to our hearts. That healing power requires being present with our pain. We can notice where we hurt inside and bring our loving awareness to those places.

Recently a student shared that in savasana over the past few weeks, the image of her recently deceased dog was coming into her mind. She said that it made her feel sad, and she wanted to know how to make it stop. "You don't," I told her, "but you can be with your sadness right now, and I'll stay here with you while you do." We stayed there while she rode those waves. As she relaxed her mind in savasana, the grieving that she had been keeping at bay by staying busy and not letting herself fully feel was rearing its head and asking for her presence. She was able to stop running and just be with her grief. Being with our feelings is how we begin to digest, assimilate, and move through them.

The experience made me revel again in the joy of experiencing the healing power of full presence. Our pure presence is the same as love. We are not always taught to hold gently those places inside of us that hurt. We try to fix it, change it, manage it, get over it, transcend it, and lots of other things that are about wanting reality to be different. It is a radical shift not to try to fix anything but to let the natural intelligence in your own presence help the hurt to be digested and move through.

When your inner hurt arises, first notice your experience. To do that, you have to slow down enough to be aware of your feelings. It's hard to notice what hurts when you are so numbed out from being busy. It's hard to feel much beyond adrenaline or fatigue.

Once you've slowed down enough to notice where it hurts, bring some love there. What does that look like for you? Like the grieving student, you can give yourself permission to bring your presence to that place where it hurts. It's not about changing this thought or aspect of yourself or wanting anything to be different than it is. Our work here is in bringing presence to those places where perhaps before we have been avoidant. We can think of the places that are stuck in being hurt as the places that feel separate from us or from a sense of resting in the divine. The love we bring reestablishes our awareness of the connection, which, in reality, was never lost.

Once you bring love to the place that needs it the most, pause. Take a few breaths. Notice how healing your own love is, flowing from your heart to wherever it hurts. Sense your innate ability to heal through love.

There is a deeper sense of personal responsibility in doing this work. There have been times in my life when I was waiting for someone else to bring love to my hurt places. That never ends well, because we each have to give ourselves that gift, and while others may be a part of the experience, ultimately, it is only ours to fully embody.

Thaddeus Golas, author of *A Lazy Man's Guide to Enlightenment*, wrote, "Whatever you are doing, love yourself for doing it. Whatever you are thinking, love yourself for thinking it. Love is the only dimension that needs to be changed. If you are not sure how it feels to be loving, love yourself for not being sure of how it feels."

His words help me to remember I can love even my resistance, and in bringing love there, I experience a softening. Something shifts, and another choice presents itself as I relate to my pain differently.

Part of coming home to yourself is creating an inner landscape that is open and transparent, where you are willing to see and be with all the parts of yourself, where no rooms in the house are boarded up, and where all of you can see the light of day.

## Journal Contemplations

+ As you bring love to hurt places, notice if you'd like some extra support in dealing with what arises. If so, would you consider seeing a therapist, coach, or spiritual advisor?
+ Do you give yourself permission to tend to all parts of your experience? If not, where did you learn that, and are you willing to shift?
+ Since all feelings flow out of the same faucet, how does your relationship to your other emotions change as a result of being present with your hurt?

# 34

## Commit to move
## your body daily

"I ain't worried/doing me tonight/A little sweat ain't never
hurt nobody!/Don't just stand there on the wall/
Everybody just move your body."
—*Beyoncé*

*I* noticed the importance of moving my body daily when I was in
my 20s and struggling with depression. The blanket of numb-
ness that was depression would slowly begin to lift when I exercised,
took a walk, did some yoga, or went dancing. It wasn't a panacea that
took everything away, but it definitely helped me to break up what felt
like a totality of heaviness. I had a similar experience after a major life
change. Movement was already a part of my daily life, but I found that
mixing it up and doing different kind of movement helped me to flow
with my feelings. My go-to movement muse at that time was Beyoncé,
because she walks her talk. Her mastery over the way she moves and

the power she exudes in her movements are a delight to witness, and serve as evidence of her commitment to move daily and with purpose.

We are consciousness, and the body is the vehicle of that consciousness. What happens to a vehicle if we leave it out in the elements, don't put gas in it, and don't start it up so the engine can run? For a really good answer, we should probably ask a mechanic, but I can venture a guess that there's rust involved and that the car doesn't work optimally if we leave it neglected for long.

The same is true for your body. The yogis have a great model of human existence that says consciousness animates the body in the form of prana, or life force energy. When these energies are moving optimally in five main directions, we have a sense of feeling balanced. The yoga postures are designed to remove energetic blockages and promote the balanced flow of our life force.

In Ayurveda, a healthy person is described as "One who is established in Self, who has balanced primary life force, balanced digestive fire, properly formed tissues, proper elimination of wastes, well-functioning bodily processes, whose mind, soul, and senses are full of bliss."

Think of how you feel when you're exercising daily. Does your experience more closely match that definition of a healthy person than when you are more sedentary? Do you have more energy, feel like your body is working well, experience an improved mood, and enjoy a healthy appetite? Of course, Ayurveda is a whole science in itself, and the teachings do not say that exercise alone is the driver of health. But daily movement is definitely beneficial and a step in the right direction.

Get creative! Moving your body doesn't have to mean traditional exercise like running outside or on the treadmill (although that does light some people up). My go-tos are walking, doing yoga, dancing, and riding my bike. Do what gets you moving. Why? We get stagnant, and then we don't feel good in our bodies, which leads to making choices that keep us feeling outside of ourselves so we can avoid our discomfort. It's like letting your house get so messy that you can't stand to be there, so you start paying to live in a hotel. That would be crazy, right? But that's exactly what we do when we ignore our bodies.

You can choose to open the door to your home. Tidy up a bit. And then, maintain. That's where the commitment comes in. Did you shudder at the word "commitment"? Never fear. Commitment doesn't have to be scary. It is a gathering of your energy and will behind a specific action. There's no inherent burden in committing, but there is a purposeful collection and direction of energy and will. Committing to moving your body every day is just marshaling your energy and will around caring for the vehicle that houses your consciousness.

Notice, there's nothing in this chapter about what your body should look like. Nothing about a size, shape, or image to try to attain. That kind of judgment is exactly what contributes to many of us not wanting to come home to ourselves. It puts a value on what the home should look like, rather than the level of love and peace that exists inside.

Our bodies and minds are linked, and what we do with one impacts the other, since they aren't separate. The body communicates with us and has tons of wisdom to share. But we can't hear that wisdom if we are disconnected from ourselves. Moving daily is a way to come home.

Whichever form of movement you've chosen, do it with your full presence. Afterward, take a few deep breaths and pause. Observe your experience, paying attention to your body, your breath, and your mind. What form did your expression of movement take, and how did that impact your mood, your thoughts, and the quality of your awareness? Enjoy it!

# Journal Contemplations

- The yogic sages broke all energy down into three main forms: Tamas, the energy of form and inertia; Rajas, the energy of movement and excitement; and Sattva, the energy of light and clarity. What mixture of these three qualities did the form of movement you chose move you into?

- Over the course of the week, notice how short bursts of movement impact your day. How is that experience different from longer bursts of movement fewer times a week?

- Does your resistance take the form of negative stories, busyness, or self-criticism? How can you move through that?

# 35

## Leave one day completely unscheduled. Notice and honor the creative impulses that arise

"Ideas are driven by a single impulse: to be made manifest."
—*Elizabeth Gilbert*

Each of us has an inner wisdom. The yogis called it dhi—the inner knowing that lives within us. It is the light of our soul, which reflects divine energy. A creative spark exists in us that wants to be expressed and needs space for that expression. While this creative principle is honed through attention-focusing processes such as meditation, it can also present itself to us when we aren't grasping for it. To wit: the amazing shower revelation, the answer to a problem that comes as you are taking a walk and your mind is empty, the idea that leaps into your awareness right as you're falling asleep. When I'm in writing mode, I wake up writing, or sometimes daydreaming turns into a fully formed idea for a project. The common theme in these examples is that the mind wasn't dedicated to an engaging task and was allowed to wander.

In addition to enjoying these randomly appearing flashes of knowing, we can choose to make space in our schedules for the creative impulse to express itself. For a time period of your choosing, I invite you to take the opportunity of leaving one day a week totally unscheduled. Based on the type of job you have, this may be a weekday or a weekend. Of course, you have chores and errands that must be done, but do your best to shuffle them around so you can give yourself this day. For those of you with children, imagine the fun you'll have inviting them to embrace an unscheduled day with wonder and curiosity.

When you wake up on your unscheduled day, instead of trotting out your giant to-do list, turn your awareness inward, and follow the impulses that arise. You may find this experience is quite surprising. First, notice when the impulse arises to eat. Have you had the experience of waking up and eating because that's just what you do to start the day? Leave the space to notice the exact moment when you feel hunger and then the exact moment when the impulse to feed yourself arises. And as you follow that impulse, notice any effect on your enjoyment of eating.

After you've completed this energetic cycle of noticing an impulse, following it through, and observing your experience, pause. Take a few breaths. Leave space for the next impulse. This is an exercise in deep listening to yourself. For many of us, it's a forgotten skill because we are overscheduled and addicted to busyness. We follow our calendar, not our heart. But forgotten skills can be relearned.

When listening for and then following impulses, it's important to bring nonjudgmental awareness to whatever arises. I remember talking to a friend about how much fun this was, and she said she was scared to try it because she thought the impulses wouldn't be ones that were helpful. I shared that, in my experience, harmful impulses didn't enter my awareness—rather, different forms of expression arose.

I felt the impulse to paint, dance, laugh, call a friend, take a walk, lie down and breathe, paint my toes, write a story, or volunteer. Having the space to let my mind roam and to hear how expression wanted to come through me has been a beautiful practice. Because I committed to nonjudgmental awareness, if an impulse arose to try something that I had told myself I wasn't good at, I noticed the thought and followed the impulse anyway. I have been surprised at what has come forth and as a result have come to know myself as a creative being.

Part of coming home to yourself is having the space to know what's in that home. Unscheduled days create space for the deepest aspects of yourself to make themselves known and to be expressed.

## Journal Contemplations

+ How can following your impulses become an exercise in trusting yourself?
+ What is it about following your impulses that helps you to experience the cocreation between the eternal and changeable aspects of yourself?
+ How do you feel in the pause between cycles of hearing the impulse, following through, and listening for the next one to arise?

# 36

# Drink a cup of warm water with lemon or lime and raw honey each morning

"Water before a meal is nectar. It replenishes fluids
and encourages juicy digestive organs."
—*Dr. Vasant Lad*

*W*arm water with lemon or lime and raw honey is a sweet "I love you" to your digestive system. Part of coming home to yourself is feeling good in your body, and it's hard to have that experience when your digestive system is out of whack. According to Ayurveda, warm water with lemon or lime and raw honey is a tune-up for your digestive system, because the warm water and the properties of the juice stimulate digestion and peristaltic action. The raw honey acts as a cleanser, scraping undigested food from the upper digestive tract. This beverage promotes proper elimination and digestion. If you tend to run hot, physically or in your personality, use lime instead of lemon.

According to yogic teachings, our soul is covered by five sheaths, called koshas. A great way to visualize this is as a lamp: the soul is the lightbulb, and the koshas are lampshades stacked five deep. The closest sheath to the soul is the bliss body, which is covered by the wisdom body, which is covered by the mental body, which is covered by the energy body, which is covered by the physical body.

We will have a hard time coming to rest in our true nature if these coverings are out of balance. If your digestion isn't working well and you aren't eliminating, your breath may be rough or choppy, your mood may be low, and the desire to do spiritual practice decreases. By starting the day caring for your physical body, we remove obstacles to feeling good physically, which sets the foundation to approach more balance in the depths of our being. Self-care makes it easier for us to do the things that allow us to have an experience of that part of our awareness that is eternal.

If we think of the body as the structure of our home, we want to ensure that the structure is strong, including the plumbing. Warm water with lemon or lime and raw honey is a great way to keep the pipes clean. Bringing ease into our physical experience helps us remove the physical distractions that can keep us from resting in ourselves.

I guess this is the part where we talk about elimination. No one wants to talk about poop, but many people have issues in this area. Lots of people are suffering from constipation, irritable bowel syndrome, and other elimination concerns. In my experience, one contributor to constipation was rushing around in the morning. For me, sipping warm water with lime in the morning made me slow down and get present. Slowing down and sipping allowed my body to relax, and, over time, along with some dietary and exercise changes, elimination was no longer a problem. If you are having elimination issues, the warm water with lemon or lime can be a first great step to help to get things moving and can create a pause in the rush-around that mornings can become.

So resist the urge to drink the beverage while doing a bunch of other things. After you drink the water, pause. Make time to be present while you drink this love letter to your digestive tract. Take a few deep belly breaths to help you to relax even more deeply during this practice.

## Journal Contemplations

- When you find that your digestive system is working with more ease, how does that impact how you move through the day?
- Where does your mind go during the pause? Do you ruminate, or does your mind turn to uplifting things?
- If you ruminate, can you decide on a short amount of time you will allow before you stop yourself?

# 37

# Take a "you" break for stillness and quiet twice a day

"Silence is the language of God. All else is poor translation."
—*Rumi*

Coming home to yourself is about holding your own hand. It's about tending to those aspects of yourself that need your tender, loving care. It's hard to hear your inner cry for care when the tone of your life is like a rocket ship. The divine in you begins speaking to you in a whisper. The louder your life is, the harder it will be for you to hear that divine whisper. And when the whisper goes unheeded, She gets louder and more insistent with Her invitations for you to come home to yourself. When we make time in our lives for stillness and quiet, we are setting ourselves up to be able to hear Her whisper before it becomes a cymbal blast of sickness, anxiety, depression, or another form of turmoil.

I have found taking a "me break" for stillness to be very healing, and I expanded it to more than just a few minutes. I had been burning the candle at both ends for a few years. Unresolved grief was the first thing to slow me down, and then a vitamin D deficiency left me feeling fatigued and drained. I literally couldn't rush around like I used to, so mornings became long and leisurely affairs filled with sipping tea, reading spiritual texts, and writing before work. In order to get through the week, I had to do Yoga Nidra a few times just to feel like I had the energy to work full-time and also teach yoga and meditation. All of these things conspired to lead me toward making time daily for stillness and quiet. I'm grateful for the experiences that led me to give myself this gift. I have reaped countless benefits, the most important of which was a relationship with myself that I'd never cultivated. As my energy came back, I kept the slower pace of mornings and evenings because I felt how nourishing it was for me at all levels.

The Ayurvedic sages saw that stillness also is a way to build our internal endurance and immunity (ojas). When you create time in your life for stillness and quiet, you gain more access to the inner wisdom of your body and mind. The mind, which has to digest all of the sensory impressions we take in as well as the experiences, uses stillness and quiet as fuel for assimilating wisdom from experiences and letting go of the rest.

What are your body signals for needing some "you" time? Have you noticed any physical sensations that correspond to needing to drop back into your own experience? Kathlyn Hendricks teaches a fabulous tool in her workshops called the "Loop of Awareness." Awareness oscillates between the inner world and the outer world, and we all have different speeds of this oscillation. When I first took her workshop, I realized that looping out to someone else, noticing their facial expressions, body language, and paying close attention to their response came to me quite easily. My loop of awareness was heavy on the looping out but light on the looping back in and noticing how I was feeling, responding and being with the other person. I found that I could practice noticing something outside of myself (looping out) and then bringing my awareness back into my experience (looping in). Want to play? Try this out! Notice how your loop works. Do you loop in more? Out to others more often? Can you begin to direct your loop of awareness rather than letting habit decide?

Take a "you" break for stillness and quiet twice a day. At some time in the morning and again in the evening, retreat slightly from whatever you are doing, and gather your awareness inward. Turn your mind toward the space around your heart. Breathe there, noticing sensation, any sense of light or heat, and a spreading feeling of well-being. Remain open to whatever arises. Pause, with your full presence on your inner world.

## Journal Contemplations

+ In what ways are you a friend to yourself throughout the day?
+ What are some early warning signs that you could use a "you" pause during the day?
+ When you notice these signs, what are the ways that you override the desire to pause?

# 38

## Buy lunch for a friend at work, and eat together

"Nothing—not a conversation, not a handshake, or even a hug
establishes friendship so forcefully as eating together."
—*Jonathan Safran Foer*

*E*ating together is one of life's pleasures. As we nurture our
bodies with food, it is quite delicious to nurture our souls
with companionship. And if we add to that the ability to gift that nurturing food to a friend, we've hit the trifecta.

Sharing is a way to come home to yourself. Picture a busy workday.
You've been going nonstop; you've barely had time to use the bathroom,
let alone create space for stillness. You're running on empty, and,
usually, you just wolf down some food with one hand while typing
with the other. Now your digestive system is tasked with digesting
and assimilating food and information and stress all at the same time.

Buying lunch for a friend and eating together is one way to create
a pause. Part of coming home to ourselves is making time throughout

the day to stop the momentum. If we let the momentum take over, we become like a hamster on a wheel, with consciousness flowing outward constantly and busyness as the value of the day. An act of service such as feeding someone else generates a sense of connection. Also, a good friend will reflect the best of you to yourself, as you will for them. Taking time out of our busy schedule to nurture our bodies is a great action to show that we value ourselves. And when pausing and taking in nurturing food converges with a sense of camaraderie, the resulting joyfulness is a beacon for coming home.

Relationships are healing. Being transparent is freeing. I used to have a "work persona"—one that was a little bit harder, less flexible, demanding, and curt. I started noticing, as I softened more in my "real life," how it was almost physically painful to put the armor of "Work Nicole" back on every day. One day, one of the students who took my corporate yoga class saw me in the hallway, placed her hands at her heart, and said "Namaste," like it was the most natural thing in the world. At that moment I realized, the only person splitting "Yoga Nicole" from "Work Nicole" was me. There was no separation. There was no difference. I was just acting differently out of fear that my soft side would open me up to attack or ridicule or that people would think I was weak or too "airy-fairy" to be taken seriously. But my strength has always been in being myself. The separation between the aspects of my personality was actually creating a sense of feeling weak, because I was scared someone would find out how *not* a hard ass I was. I am grateful to that student for providing a mirror that let me start to integrate the parts of myself I was keeping separate.

The invitation to take someone to lunch and to become friends or deepen the friendship is actually a step toward your own integration. Perhaps you have already integrated the different aspects of your personality, in which case the benefit is still that you create an oasis of connection in the middle of the day.

As you enjoy your friend's company, speak of uplifting things. Take a lunch-long moratorium from talking about work. Speak what's in your heart. Take a chance to let yourself be seen and to truly see another, despite being at work—a context that isn't always conducive to removing the masks that separate us. As you create this oasis for yourself and for another, pause. Notice how this space for authenticity has a spreading quality that invites you and those around you to relate more deeply.

## Journal Contemplations

+ Do you have any beliefs about letting go of compartmentalizing and being authentic with a colleague?
+ How do you feel about giving yourself permission to pause in a context that supports nonstop work?
+ Do you feel more connected to your own heart after you give something to another?

# 39

# Wake up at dawn
# to meditate

"The healthy person should get up (from bed) during brahma
muhurta, to protect his life."
—*Ashtanga Hridayam, Vol. I, 2:1*

*A*yurveda teaches us that in nature, and in us, qualities such
as heaviness, density, and stillness, pervade the hours of 6 to
10 in the morning and evening. By waking up before that time, around
dawn, to sit in silence or meditation, we capitalize on the natural clarity
that precedes the sturdiness and solidity of the postdawn hours of the day.

Full disclosure: I have had to train myself to be a morning person.
I'm not. I like to laze around in bed snuggling my beloved, and even
when I'm sleeping alone, I like to log roll into my comforter so I feel
like I'm hugged in. When I started studying Ayurveda, the idea of
getting up when it's cold and dark was totally unappealing to me. But
I love experiments, and I believe in practicing what I preach, so I met
myself in the middle and started getting up at 6:30. Not quite dawn

but not 9 AM either. And the quietness of the house at that time, the solitude—in that busy city sounds aren't yet so apparent—these things set the conditions for me to really be with myself. They set the conditions for the desire for meditation to arise. And over time, it became more natural to wake up before 6 AM. Not to say that some mornings aren't a struggle or that I don't occasionally succumb to the joy of staying in bed a bit later, but I find that the benefits of being early to bed and early to rise outweigh any downside. There is no difference between the sacred and the mundane, but sometimes we need a little bit of silence in order to feel the holiness of living—making the morning coffee, feeding our families, or heading into the job that pays for our lives.

There is a deep silence at dawn. It's as if the world is wrapped in a blanket of stillness. This is an amazing time to meditate. Your mind is at its easiest, the world is quiet, and, according to the sages, this is the time when we can most easily hear the wisdom of the divine. Let the silence of the world around you usher you into the silence of your heart. Our essence is fullness. The *Isha Upanishad*, a yogic text, tells us of our true nature:

| | |
|---|---|
| All this is full | *Om purnam adah* |
| All that is full | *Purnam idam* |
| From fullness, fullness comes | *Purnat purnam udachyate* |
| When fullness is taken from fullness | *Purnasya purnam adaya* |
| Fullness yet remains | *Purnam evavashishyate* |

In the early morning hours, the airy and ethereal qualities of light, clear, and subtle bring us closer to an experience of our fullness. The mental cacophony of likes and dislikes, jumbled thoughts, and fear hasn't quite started yet. Take advantage of that, and create a space in your home and in your schedule to bask in your own fullness. Experience the part of your consciousness that is full of abundance, always whole, and always complete, regardless of what is occurring in the world of form.

This fullness is your true nature whether you're happy or sad, whether life is a struggle or dripping with ease, whether you feel connected or very much alone. This fullness is your home. Come home to yourself, and touch your inner light just before the sun's light touches the earth.

If you do not have experience with meditation, there are great apps and recordings that offer guided meditations to assist you in starting this new practice, such as Rod Stryker's *Meditations for Life*. After your desired time of meditation, pause for a while before moving into your day. Enjoy the bounty of having taken the time to expand your consciousness.

## Journal Contemplations

+ How does waking up at dawn impact the quality of awareness with which you move into your day?
+ How do you experience your innate sense of fullness?
+ In what ways do periods of silence support you?

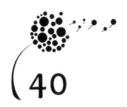

# 40

# When you feel an emotion, pause, acknowledge it to yourself, and breathe into the place where you feel it in your body

"Between stimulus and response, there is a space.
In that space is our power to choose our response.
In our response lies our growth and our freedom."
—*Viktor E. Frankl*

*E*motions, like thoughts, are fluctuations of the mind. Our emotions are chemical responses to our thoughts and perceptions. We can see anger as a natural response to perceived trespass, sadness as a natural response perceived loss, fear as a natural response to perceived danger, and joy as a response to perceived connection with our source.

Often we don't realize that there's a short gap between feeling an emotion and reacting to it. Because we aren't aware of these few seconds, when we feel angry, we may blurt a curse at a fellow driver. We feel sad and may grasp for something to help us feel okay amid the sense of loss. We feel fear, and we may avoid the source of the fear.

There is a different choice. Rather than react, we can pause, take a breath, and get present. How can we know when we're in the grip of an emotion? They are accompanied by body sensations. We can train ourselves to access our body's wisdom by bringing awareness to physical sensation. Sadness sensations are often felt in the throat or upper chest, fear deep in the belly, anger in the back of the neck and upper back, and joy all over the body. So the next time you notice a big emotion, pause. Observe the sensations in your body. Place your attention on the sensations and breathe with what you feel. Stay with it until the intensity of the feeling moves through you. This is not easy, but it is a skill that is useful in helping us to manage our reactivity.

Last week, my husband said something to me, and I felt sad and scared. I noticed I felt my belly clench and heaviness across my chest. I breathed into these sensations and brought my full presence to them. My presence made me feel like I was holding my own hand as these emotions passed through. In not abandoning myself while I felt my feelings, I made it safe for myself not to be reactive. Instead, I was available to respond by saying, "Hey, when I heard you say that, I felt sad and scared. It reminded me of a time when I felt really judged and dismissed." As we communicated more deeply, we understood much better where the other person was coming from. It isn't always easy, but like anything else, with practice, it is achievable in most situations.

An integral part of coming home to yourself is a willingness to be present with whatever arises in your experience. I remember hearing my spiritual teacher say, "A master hides nothing from herself." Sometimes there are emotions that weren't safe to feel when we were growing up. Either our parents didn't know how to handle them or didn't teach us how to deal with them skillfully. It's so important to turn toward those now, so we don't keep invalidating our experience by stuffing or denying how we feel. It's only by shining the light of our awareness into those dark places that we can begin to discern what is true.

We can stop hiding from ourselves. We don't have to believe everything we think or act on every emotion that arises, but we do benefit from observing these mental ripples and holding ourselves lightly while they glide through. It's the presence we bring that allows the gliding through of the feeling to occur, just as the lack of presence makes us reactive and evokes behaviors that keep us stuck in a cycle of disconnecting from ourselves.

I've been taught that all feeling flows out of the same faucet. When I opened to the full flowering of my feelings, even the ones that were hard for me to presence, I began feeling more access to my innate flowing of joy. In working with life-coaching clients, the fear that comes up the most for people is that they will be overwhelmed by their emotions, as if once they start crying, they will never stop. It's important to cultivate the witness, which, from a yoga perspective, is our ability to be present with our experience while still being able to observe it. If you have deep trauma, this work is best done with the support of a professional. If that is not the case for you, the act of cultivating presence without identifying with the changing state of the mind can help you to sustain steadiness in the presence of large waves of emotion.

## Journal Contemplations

+ How do you feel when you slow your mind down enough to presence the gap between the emotion arising and your response?
+ Do you have judgments around specific emotions? How can you release these?
+ Do you feel more expansive when you allow the full range of feeling? If not, what happens for you?

# 41

## Move to your favorite song without wearing any clothes

*"Being naked approaches being revolutionary;*
*going barefoot is mere populism."*
*— John Updike*

*H*ow often do we create a space for ourselves to drop the armor within? We often think of vulnerability as being between two people. But we also build walls within our own minds and hearts in an effort to protect ourselves. When is the last time you opened those inner vaults to yourself? When is the last time you opened your eyes to some part of yourself from which you try to hide, and let your gaze be soft so you could bathe those tender parts of you in love?

I have found that when I really feel stuck, one of the best ways to access the opportunity to be vulnerable and shine love on myself instead of judgment is to dance in the nude. It's a way to access my wildness, my deep spirit, my freedom to move how and when I want in ways that feel good to me. We've already discussed the power of dance in this book, but the up-level of nudity adds a deeper level of letting go. Perhaps because it's just you, without the cover of clothing and any personas that lurk in the way that we dress. It's pure, unvarnished *you*.

For many of us, nudity is not the most comfortable feeling, as we may not be fully comfortable with our body or with the way that we move. We may be so disconnected from moving our bodies that just thinking about moving to music brings up a cacophony of judges, let alone doing it with no clothes on. But once we move through that fear, there is a sense of freedom that emerges, as you begin to move in ways that feel playful and fun and sexy for you, as you let your body express without the covering of clothes, as you feel your limbs flowing through the air unadorned, and unbound.

After you dance, pause and breathe. Notice the sensations in your body, and that sense of joy, acceptance, and flowing energy. That's how the divine manifests in you.

If your inner critic does rise up to condemn a body part or a way of moving, you can choose to see that as an opportunity for you to pause and bring your breath and awareness to the place that you are judging. I learned a tool from Gay Hendricks that is quite effective here. Bring into your mind someone that you know you love. Feel the palpable sense of love you have for that person. See that love like a covering of light, and then let that light and love encompass the part of yourself that you're judging. Feel the shift from rejection to love, which is acceptance.

We all have those tender spots, those places where we do not want to go because we find it so hard to accept. This doesn't have to be a pattern we leave undisturbed. We can make it a practice to shine our light on those places, a light filled with love and acceptance. Part of coming home to ourselves is to make sure there are no rooms in the house that we have boarded up, stopped heating, left vacant. We are here to fully occupy ourselves, inhabiting our bodies and minds with the gift of our presence. We drain our own energy when we have places within us where we don't let ourselves go.

Let the dance usher you into this deeper relationship with yourself, one in which you are willing to hold your own hand just like you would a friend's if they needed to feel loved and accepted.

## Journal Contemplations

+ How often are you vulnerable with yourself?
+ What is your experience of turning love toward the parts of you that you usually judge?
+ How does moving your body without wearing clothes open up new experiences of intimacy with yourself?

# 42

# Eat more foods that contribute to your felt sense of aliveness, and slowly remove from your diet those that dampen your energy

"Let food be thy medicine, thy medicine shall be thy food."
—*Hippocrates*

*W*hat we eat has a direct impact on the quality of our minds and the way we feel physically, hence, the old maxim "You are what you eat." From an Ayurvedic perspective, the food we take into our bodies ultimately becomes the substance that builds our tissues. It stands to reason that it can only be beneficial to bring more awareness toward what we put into our mouths. Further, when our bodies first start to go out of balance, we crave foods that will bring us back into balance. So if we cultivate a deep inner listening as it relates to eating, and if we aren't too deep into our imbalances, we can start to experience food as medicine because our cravings will be healthy ones. Alternately, once we have made it a habit to eat in ways that decrease our energy, those cravings will serve to keep us in our imbalance. So it is to our advantage to bring our exquisite presence to what and how we eat!

Mindful eating is practiced in many spiritual circles, and, in the Himalayan Tradition, eating can be viewed as its own spiritual practice. If we view eating as an offering to the divine within us, seeing the food itself and the act of eating it as sacred, and feeling the digestive fire in our belly as the sacred flames that consume the offering of food, the whole experience of eating changes. We can choose to bring the sublime into everything we do, and by bringing that energy into the act of eating, we start to turn our consciousness more and more toward an experience of the eternal.

As we shift our view of eating, it becomes important to turn our awareness to how the offerings that we are giving to that sacred fire within make us feel. When we slow down enough to notice the body sensations accompanied by eating, we begin to observe which foods enliven us and which foods do not. According to yogic philosophy, all matter has a mixture of three different qualities: Tamas, which is inertia, Rajas, which is activity, and Sattva, which is light. This means all *foods* can be categorized this way as well. Tamasic foods are foods that are heavy and ground (or dull, in large quantities) our energy. Alcohol is tamasic, which makes sense because it's a depressant. Rajasic foods are stimulating. Think of how you feel when you eat a hot pepper or a sharp, aged cheese. Sattvic foods are easy to digest, like vegetables, basmati rice, or ghee (clarified butter). The aftereffect of eating sattvic foods is lightness of being. Our minds may feel more clear, less dull, and not as racy when our diet is filled with foods that are more sattvic. An easy way to remember sattvic foods is to see them in terms of their closeness to the sun, such as fruit.

Part of being at home in yourself is giving yourself exquisite attention. When applied to the act of eating, you can use your body awareness to choose more foods that contribute to your felt sense of aliveness and slowly let go of eating those that dampen your energy.

Foods that make you feel light and alive contribute to lightness of being, mentally and physically. And your inner attention will help you distinguish between foods that bring you aliveness and foods that give you a sugar rush or an adrenaline hit, which are poor substitutes for the real deal and, ultimately, make you feel drained. Bringing awareness to the aftereffect of foods will help us to choose foods that light us up. We also gain a sense of when we actually feel full. And we might notice when we are eating as a way to deal with emotion as opposed to when our body needs fuel.

So the next time you sit down to eat, notice what lights you up. After your meal, pause. Breathe into your experience of eating with more awareness. Feeling aliveness means our life force (prana) is flowing well, and when prana flows with ease, that sense of inner well-being draws us inward, and we see there is no place like our true home.

## Journal Contemplations

- Can you feel the difference, based on the sensations in your body, between healthy food cravings and food cravings that will crash your energy?
- How do you experience the impact the way you eat has on your mood?
- How might you titrate your dietary shifts so that you are slowly letting go of foods that feel draining and slowly adding more foods that feel balancing?

# 43

## Notice where you hold yourself back. Ask yourself, "What would I do if no one was watching?" Take steps toward living full out in those places

"The purpose of life, after all, is to live it, to taste experience
to the utmost, to reach out eagerly and without fear
for newer and richer experience."
—*Eleanor Roosevelt*

*I*t is easy to forget that we are a reflection of the ultimate reality of truth, consciousness, and bliss. We are quick to identify with the changeable rather than the changeless. In truth, we are both. If we are vast consciousness wanting to experience the many flavors of existence, one of those being you, then you owe it to yourself to be as bright as possible, fully living into your experience of being human.

What stops you from being full out? Where do you contract when your whole being is inviting you to expand? There are myriad reasons why we hold ourselves back, from familial and social conditioning to fear of failure or even a perceived lack of resources. These beliefs and fears are what we use to justify the slowing down or even stopping of our full expression in life. What would our lives look like if we released those shackles? Much of our fear comes from attachment, in that we think there is something we would have to give up if we were to start living full out. Some fear losing social status, others think they'd make less money, and others are scared to fail or don't feel their life is set up for them to choose. But what if the things we are scared we would lose are just a gateway to a fullness of experience that we haven't yet encountered?

In my own example, I've often have had the impulse to smile. Many times, just walking down the street, I have felt a natural connection to a deep sense of well-being and joy inside of me. But I thought it was weird to walk around smiling, so when I felt myself smile, I would switch my face back into a neutral position. I noticed when I was on retreat, I gave myself permission to spontaneously smile or laugh, but in life at home, I shut myself down. I decided one day that, if I wanted my life to feel the way it did when I was on retreat, I had to allow myself to be the me that I was when I was at a training. And an easy step toward doing that was to allow myself to smile. The impact was so beautiful. I felt more like myself, and since smiles are contagious, I noticed that wherever I went, people were often smiling back at me. Sometimes they would even tell me that seeing me smile made them smile. In facing that fear of being judged and allowing my inner state to shine through, I opened to more connection with people and a deeper connection to myself based on my authentic experience no longer being sublimated.

When you live fully into yourself, you are also being of service to the whole because you're creating a model for someone to see, and perhaps they give themselves permission to live more full out.

We are not here to hide and shrink and stay small, nor are we here to get puffed up with ego and lord our power over other people. There is a sweet spot of being toe to toe with life, of expanding ourselves to our personal edges, of embracing our true nature of limitlessness, so consciousness within us can have its fullest expression through us. Part of being at home wherever you are is rising up and touching the most alive place in you. It's letting your expression and your actions come from that core light and joy that is you and that is in you.

## Journal Contemplations

+ What impulses for full-out living arise that scare you?
+ How can you add more breath while presencing your fear?
+ How do you respond to impulses to express, expand, create, love, or give?

# 44

# Chant or sing the names
# of the Divine

"Chanting is a way of getting in touch with yourself. It's an opening of the heart and letting go of the mind and thoughts. It deepens the channel of grace, and it's a way of being present in the moment."
—*Krishna Das*

Much of our pain in life can be traced back to feeling separate from our source and forgetting that we are always connected. This leads to feelings of isolation, from people, from family, from yourself. A deep sense of loneliness prevails when our connection to the deeper truths of life feels severed. Everything starts to look dark, and, in that darkness, we begin our retreat, first from ourselves, using numbing substances and behaviors so we don't feel that disconnect. Once we feel disconnected from ourselves, the outside world starts to look and feel unsafe, and as we interact with the world as an unsafe place, we feel less and less connected to nature, to friends, to family, to our community. Depression can set in, and, without healthy coping skills, life can feel pretty bleak.

Having dealt with depression for much of my 20s, I was grateful for being introduced to yoga and meditation, two practices that helped me to loosen my attachment to a pervasive inner sense of separation. At the beginning of that journey, I remember being invited to a kirtan with Krishna Das. Kirtan is call-and-response singing, where the person leading sings part of a mantra or a song meant to invoke an aspect of the divine, and, after listening, the audience sings the same lines back. It can be done in person, and there are also recordings that you can listen to so you have the same experience outside of the context of a live show.

That night, I didn't know who all of the names were referring to, and I was very concerned with getting it right, which, of course, took me out of the experience. At one point, I forgot to be self-conscious, and I just sang the words back. I felt my heart lift, and, as I kept singing, I felt my body fill with light, which led to an overwhelming burst of joy in my chest, accompanied by tears coming out of my eyes. That light felt like it reestablished a connection to an inner luminosity that I hadn't felt in a very long time.

Chanting is an age-old practice, found in many traditions, from Buddhism, to Judaism, to Sufism, to the monks of Christian religions. If we think about sound as the sense closest to pure spirit, it follows that, as we sing the names of the divine, we are led to a palpable sense of inner alignment with the divine flame that is within us. In terms of music to try out, Krishna Das is a good place to start, and there are plenty of artists from all traditions making devotional music in ancient languages.

On a physiologic level, chanting is related to regulating the breath. In order to chant the long mantras we have to lengthen our inhale, which is known to build prana, our life force. A lengthened exhalation also activates the parasympathetic nervous system, which helps us to rest and digest.

Try it! Download a kirtan song, sing the call and response verses until the end, and then pause. Melt into your own heart.

When we chant, we build our light, and that light can lead us home to ourselves. There have been many names for that light over the centuries, and our singing of the names that represent that light helps us to attune to it more deeply.

## Journal Contemplations

+ Which wisdom tradition appeals to you in terms of singing the names? Bonus: you don't have to limit yourself to the one you grew up with, and you can try out other traditions.
+ What's your relationship to a sense of the divine within you?
+ What blocks to experiencing that inner divinity need to be released in order for you to enjoy this practice?

# 45

# Watch your favorite film
# (no multitasking allowed)

"Film as dream, film as music. No art passes our conscience
in the way film does, and goes directly to our feelings, deep down
into the dark rooms of our souls."
—*Ingmar Bergman*

One of my favorite films is *Almost Famous*. When I watch
it, I feel like I've entered a realm that makes perfect sense
and all is right with the world. It has everything I like in it: amazing
music, characters who care so much about something that they're
willing to risk everything, Philip Seymour Hoffman (who always
reminds me of the depths of being human), characters who don't fit
in to the world at large but form their own family, and characters
whose relationships leave each other changed. I think it's that last
bit that resonates with me the most—by being yourself, however
weird, creative, wild, sexy, nerdy, obsessive, selfish, and loving
that version of you is in the moment, when you allow yourself to

be fully seen, it gives everyone around you the permission to step into their authenticity.

What reminder does your favorite film gift you? What does it put you in touch with, deep within? Put on the movie, and watch it without multitasking. If you're checking your phone, cooking dinner, and intermittently picking up the iPad, your lack of attention may cause you to miss the message. It's your full presence that allows the seeping in of whatever message you need to hear.

Art has always made us see ourselves and the world through new eyes, and a quality film is no different. It doesn't always have to be super deep. You might like something as campy as *The Sandlot*, because the belly laughs you feel while watching that movie are just what you needed to remind you to put more in your life that helps you to touch joy. The tears you shed when watching your sappiest romantic comedy, such as my go-to rom com, *Love Actually*, may be just the thing you need to help you feel the deep longing or sadness you've been avoiding. If you want to go more highbrow and are looking for big emotion, anything by Paul Thomas Anderson will do. I find that whenever I feel stuck in a particular emotion, if I watch a movie that evokes that emotion, I go deep enough into it that I come out on the other side.

It may seem counterintuitive that a form of entertainment could bring you home to yourself, but, to me, it's all about intention. If your intention is to check out and escape, then that's what you'll create. But if your intention is to be with yourself, most anything done with complete presence can take you there.

A good film can also uncover hidden yearning. Watching any film on creativity reminds me of how much I enjoy creating. There's nothing like enjoying a film and then going to my computer to write something. Art inspires more art.

Your turn. After you watch your favorite movie, pause and breathe. Notice how you feel. Did you choose something that lifted you up? Did the film move you emotionally? Taking an opportunity to relax and just be is an effective pattern-interrupt for habitual busyness.

## Journal Contemplations

* Watching a good movie is a form of play. What's your relationship to making time in your life for play?
* What are the qualitative differences between using an experience to escape and using it to be more present with yourself?
* How does the movie you chose help you to see into your own heart more deeply?

# 46

# Book a trip, and leave your phone at home

"Travel and change of place impart new vigor to the mind."
—*Seneca*

Sometimes the easiest way to come home to ourselves is to see the world with fresh eyes. When we travel, we can leave behind the daily tasks, roles, and requirements that keep us so busy we may not find time to go within. Everything is shaken up when we travel, from our schedule, to our surroundings, to the food we are eating, and the people with whom we are spending time. Within this shake-up, there is an opportunity to step into aspects of ourselves that we haven't explored.

Your trip can be as far away or as close to home as you have the means to achieve. There's even a service called "Pack Up + Go," which will ask you for your budget, travel dates, and travel preferences, before booking a trip for you to a destination that meets your requirements.

When you're on your trip, be sure to leave your phone at home, or, if you have people you must check in with, set a daily screen-time limit for yourself. Our life is like a stream, and the habits and activities we have and do are what keeps that stream moving in a particular direction. A vacation is a pause in the stream that can reroute us in a fresh and purposeful direction. If you go away, but you're still checking email, answering calls, and reading social media, the break in the momentum of your habits cannot occur.

Rather than seeing your trip as a way to run away from stress, you can frame it as a way for you to run toward yourself. Before you leave, make a list of the self-care habits you'd like to cultivate, but haven't made time to do. While you're on your vacation, give yourself that space to try a few. Make time for exercise, journaling, contemplations, or reading. Make time for doing nothing and letting your mind roam, or for exploring your surroundings, with no particular aim in mind. Pause, slowing the march of time, making space in your head and in your heart.

A few years ago, I took a yoga vacation to the south of France. For once, I didn't bring a ton of spiritual books (okay—I brought two, but I am who I am), and I had no project to complete. I woke up with the sun and journaled. I oiled my body and meditated. I explored a different style of yoga and saw that I could practice in a way that was unfamiliar to me but had its benefits. I explored the southern French terrain with friends, alternating between sharing laughs and being deep in my own head and heart. I tried new foods and luxuriated in the wine the region had to offer. I read a book by Hafiz and a new translation of the *Yoga Sutras*. It was magnificent. My only agenda was to practice and to have fun. I didn't bring some deep thing to work through or to process. And the outcome was amazing. The full relaxation into that experience taught me that my internal commitment to growth pulses through my life.

Creating spaciousness for just being is one of the best ways to come home to yourself. The sense of wonder and curiosity that we bring to new surroundings is also available to us in our daily lives. Stop the momentum of your life, take a break from the roles that you play, and just allow yourself to be. In that moment, in that release of attachment to all that is changeable, you touch that changeless part of you that is always there, eternally watching and supporting you across the spectrum of experience in your life.

## Journal Contemplations

- Do you find that, when you go on a trip, the days are just as full as when you're home? How does it feel to give yourself some unscheduled time?
- When your external surroundings change, what shifts happen in your internal landscape?
- What aspects of yourself emerged on your trip that you want to bring home with you and integrate into your daily life?

# 47

## Go to bed and wake up at the same time each day for a month. Notice the results

"O magic sleep! O comfortable bird,
That broodest o'er the troubled sea of the mind.
Till it is hush'd and smooth!"
—*John Keats*

*I*t can be extremely healing to align ourselves with the rhythms of nature. The cycles of nature are consistent, while many of us have schedules that are quite variable. While there is beauty in variety, and changeability *is* one of the joys of being human, adding some grounding routine to our lives also serves a positive function.

Daily routine is the anchor from which the many flavors of your being can flourish and be expressed. Waking up and going to bed at the same time every day can help to regulate your system. As an Ayurvedic Health Counselor, I have had clients come to me for help with sleep issues. Difficulty falling asleep, difficulty staying asleep, and not enough sleep are the three complaints I hear the most. Good sleep requires powering down, and many of us have forgotten how to do that. Nature can help us. Observe the beauty of twilight, as the sun is starting to set, noticing how the shadows get longer as the day dims into night. Observe the beauty of dawn, as the earth begins to wake up, light spreading across the sky and birds happily chirping to start the day. We can align with these rhythms to our personal benefit, and in reestablishing our link to natural rhythms, we can start to rest in our true nature with more ease.

We need to create our own personal twilight. What habits do you have that create the powering down of your nervous system, the gathering in of your energy, the quieting down of your mind in order to prepare for the night's sleep? Try to begin your twilight around 9 pm with the turning off of your electronic devices. Attempt to turn your mind toward peaceful things as you do a few gentle yoga postures or breathing exercises. Fill your mind with spirit by reading some spiritual passages before bed. Rub your feet with some oil to soothe your body and taxed nervous system.

When we sleep, the body heals. Toxins are being gathered from the system and collected as waste for elimination. The fire of the mind is digesting all of the day's experiences, throwing images of those we can't digest onto the screen of our minds as we dream. Sleep is a huge part of our system being balanced.

In the morning, you can create your own dawn. When the birds start chirping, you can begin to wake up, stretching and noticing what your body needs to start the day. You can begin to, in the immortal words of James Brown, "get on the good foot" by offering a prayer of gratitude before stepping out of bed. After offering the gratitude, pause, acknowledging the fullness with which you are starting your day. Let your morning take on a slow burn, like the rising of the sun.

By aligning with nature through going to bed and waking up at the same time each day, creating a ritual to help sustain that routine, we create a bookend of positive, loving attention for ourselves at the end of each day. These bookends become the structure on which our home rests. When that structure feels strong, we have faith in ourselves, faith in our body and mind's ability to heal, and faith in the energy that sustains the rhythms of Mother Nature.

## Journal Contemplations

+ What three things would help you to create your own personal twilight? Your personal dawn?
+ Does resistance arise to adding more routine to your day? How do you move through that?
+ How does the anchor of routine create more spaciousness in your life?

# 48

# Treat yourself to a massage

"Our bodies communicate to us clearly and specifically,
if we are willing to listen."
—*Shakti Gawain*

Nurturing touch can be one of the easiest and most pleasurable ways to come home to yourself. Let's try it. For a
few moments, take a seat. Place one hand on your chest and the other
hand on top, close your eyes, and take five deep belly breaths. Do you
feel more centered?

The skin is your largest organ, so tending to it through comforting
touch immediately draws your awareness back into your body. While
self-massage is definitely a transformative practice, so is receiving a
massage. Especially if we are used to being the one offering care, it can
be a revolutionary act to allow ourselves to be cared for by another.

The residue of thoughts and emotions that we hold onto during the
day can be seen in the tightness of our muscles and connective tissue.

Massage is a great way to digest and release on a physical level. It can be hard to hear and respond to your body's wisdom when tension and stress interfere or dampen the signals your body is giving you. Massage appeals to all of the senses—from the luxurious deliciousness of the essential oils, to the ambiance of the massage room, and the softness of the music playing.

For those of you who tense up at the thought of a stranger (albeit highly trained) touching your body, you may opt to ask for one from your beloved. Each stroke of your skin and muscles is a silent love letter whispered by your beloved and received by you at a very tangible level. And offering to massage your partner is a great way to give back.

Whether you're partnered or not, do you often receive healing, nonsexual touch? When I was single and lived alone, one of the first things I noticed was how little touch was in my life. If I didn't hang out with a friend that day and just went to work and came home, a whole day could go by without physical contact. I noticed that I craved physical connection and wanted to make sure I wasn't seeking it in ways that wouldn't serve me. If you are going through a period of life in which physical touch isn't available, massage can be a great way to have healthy and healing physical contact.

A massage reminds you of the joy of being. There is nothing to do but to lie there, breathe, and be. And hopefully, enjoy. When we get a massage, we are practicing receiving. After the massage, pause. Don't just hop up and resume your regular activities. Take five deep belly breaths and be in the experience. In that stillness, take a moment to appreciate that you took the time to come home to yourself in this way.

Treating yourself to a massage is an investment in yourself. Whether you pay for a massage or ask for one from a partner, you're investing your time and money in self-care. There are often massage schools or community co-ops where you can find affordable treatments.

You're treating your body as a temple worthy of exquisite care, as a vessel to which you want to come home. Our minds can easily trivialize self-care as indulgent, especially when life gets busy, but when we commit to at least one action a day that brings us home to ourselves, that experience of tending to our body, mind, and soul permeates our actions and lets us experience the nurturing we need. When you treat your body as divine consciousness made manifest, it is easier to experience your true nature, which is life, light, and love.

## Journal Contemplations

+ Before you get a massage, do a body scan and notice the level of body wisdom that's available to you in this state. For example, tune into the emotional centers (throat, chest, belly, back of the neck, and shoulders) and notice what's there to be observed.
+ After the massage, bring your awareness back to those same areas. What level of body wisdom is available to you now?
+ If the parts of your body where you feel the tightest could talk, what would they say?

# 49

## Say "No" to activities and people that do not support your brightest shining

"When you say 'yes' to others, make sure
you are not saying 'no' to yourself."
— *Paulo Coelho*

It's time to get practical. Take out a notebook. Make a list of the people that you spend your time with, whether it's in person, or via email or social media. Who are the people you are in contact with, and how do you feel when you're around them? Be real with yourself. Who are the friends with whom you spend time and feel the most lifted up, the most present, the most connected? Who are the people that you have around you about whom you feel neutral? Are there some people you spend time with, either in person or through other means of communication, whom you do not find enlivening? Are there any people with whom you spend time and then feel lower energy, or like you were just under attack? Write that down.

Now make a list of your activities. How do you spend your time? Which activities are rejuvenating? Which ones move you closer to expressing your purpose? Which ones put food on the table? Which ones drain your energy? Are there any activities you engage in that result in feeling diminished? Any activities that are harmful to your heart? Write these down as well.

The people we spend our time around and the things that we do create our life. Now that you can see these behaviors on paper, contemplate how they do or do not help you to live into and express your best self.

This is not about making rash decisions. It's about bringing our powers of observation to bear on how we live our life. It's about making conscious some of the likely unconscious choices we make about how we spend our time. After you make the list, let it sit for a few days. As you move through your life, bring even more awareness to how you feel during the activities you've identified as not being supportive for you. Bring exquisite attention to how you feel when you are in the presence of the people on your list.

When I've written this list, I've noticed friendships that I kept only because of their longevity. I had a desire to have people in my life who had known me a long time. But the truth is, a few of these friendships were not uplifting. We had changed enough that our core values were not the same, and that showed up in how forced it felt to try to connect. I noticed some of these friendships felt more like a drain than a joy. It was time to let them go. I'm also reminded of activities that no longer served me. As much as I love teaching yoga, having a full-time job meant that my schedule was quite full. At one point, teaching four classes a week became overwhelming, and my energy shifted toward getting through it rather than enjoying transmitting the teachings of yoga. Though I felt sad to do so, it was time to let a few classes go, so that I could live what I was teaching about self-care.

In both of these examples, I had to dig deep to find the courage to say "No" to a person or an activity. But there are other times in which the answer was more about shifting my relationship to someone or about changing the way I went about an activity. So don't fear that doing this joyful pause guarantees you have to give up something. You may just need to shift how you relate.

And yes, you may have to give something up. While doing so, you can invoke the "friendly clause," finding a way to let go or to shift your relationship to someone or something in a way that feels friendly to you and to the other person. Maybe that looks like having a conversation with another person about how you feel when you're together. Change can come from that. Maybe it looks like exploring whether an activity that feels overwhelming might not feel as overwhelming if you asked for some support.

This aspect of self-care can be tough. Sometimes being our own best friend is the work of culling out those ways of being that no longer serve us. It takes courage to be willing to say "No" to things we've previously said "Yes" to, yet the fire of our courage can also usher in new creative potentials to which we can say "Yes."

## Journal Contemplations

+ What do you need to stop doing to make more room for self-care?
+ What resistance do you have to letting go of relationships that no longer serve you?
+ In what ways do you give yourself permission to let go of what needs to be released and to make room for what wants to come your way?

# 50

# Forgive someone

"Forgiveness is not always easy. At times, it feels more painful than the wound we suffered, to forgive the one that inflicted it. And yet, there is no peace without forgiveness."
—*Marianne Williamson*

*A*t our very core, we are all made of the same stuff. According to yogic philosophy, there is an all-pervasive consciousness which gave rise to each of us, and we embody that consciousness in individual form. If that is not a context that lands for you, remember that we are all star stuff, made up of the same organic material as the stars that exist in the sky today and thousands of years ago.

It is in this context that we can discuss forgiveness. If, from a scientific *and* spiritual perspective, we are all one, then what is there that can't be forgiven? At the level as basic as our DNA, we are made from the same raw materials. So much of our suffering stems from the belief that we are not whole. Suffering begins when we see some parts of us as separate from the all-pervasive consciousness from which we can never really be separate. That is the mistake of our intellect, the effect of believing the illusion of separation over the reality. For example, the hairs on a dog's back are not separate from the dog, right? But if the hairs had individual consciousness and started to believe they were separate, that would be their experience despite the fact of reality.

Likewise, when we hold a grudge against someone, we are denying that wholeness that links all of us, causing suffering to them and also to ourselves.

One way to come home to ourselves is to forgive someone. For whatever it was and however they did it, forgive them. It's holding onto the grudge that creates the underlying false fissure of separation, which is the root cause of our suffering. Forgive them. And when we do, we forgive ourselves. We forgive ourselves at the same time that we forgive others, and we release our guilt and shame at believing the pain of separation is real. We forgive ourselves for believing that we were anything other than whole. We release the person we have forgiven back into their wholeness in our minds, and we reclaim our own. When we think some part of another is broken, on some level, we are believing that about ourselves as well.

Underneath the pain and anger that we carry is a belief that this particular thought, that specific behavior, these words, could possibly be outside of the divine. Those thoughts, words, or actions may not have been skillful, but they cannot be separate from the source from which they came. Nothing can ever be separate from its source, because that source is inherently a part of the composition of that which evolves from it.

Since we all stem from the same source, whether we call it the Big Bang or Divine Mother or God or energy or a cosmic soup, we are That, and if we are That, then the person we need to forgive is That also. When we release them, we release ourselves and become free. From that freedom, we can choose to come home to ourselves, to create a life filled with the practices that keep us in a state of remembrance of our true nature. We see that divine source in us and in every other human, in the birds and the trees, and in the very ground we are walking on. We come home to the experience of being spirits in human form, touching the joyfulness inherent in each moment of life, which we can rest in when we feel the thrum of that divinity that is everything and everywhere.

Forgive. It doesn't mean the circumstances that require forgiving were right and good. It also doesn't mean you need to invite the person back into your life. It just means you choose not to identify with the hurt any longer. You know the person you feel harmed you is much more than their actions, and that the reason you're both in pain is that you both forgot. Let your forgiveness be the first step toward remembrance.

## Journal Contemplations

* Does forgiveness feel empowering to you, or disempowering? Where did you learn to see it that way?
* How does forgiveness make more room for your own inner light?
* How does coming home to yourself feel when you release blame and indignation?

# 51

# Take a day trip
# to a new place

"The big question is whether you are going to be able
to say a hearty 'Yes' to your adventure."
—*Joseph Campbell*

*A*uthor and mystic Joseph Campbell is known in part for his mapping out of the archetypal narrative pattern in his book *The Hero's Journey.* Call into your mind the stories that have lasted through the ages, and you may recognize the structure. According to Campbell, "A hero ventures forth from the world of common day into a region of supernatural wonder: fabulous forces are there encountered, and a decisive victory is won: the hero comes back from this mysterious adventure with the power to bestow boons on his fellow man."

We may feel closer to such a journey when we set out on an epic trip or a retreat. And even though Campbell isn't talking only about the journey in the physical sense, we can still access this energy any time we travel. It can be tough to access a sense of wonder when we are in our routine. The embrace of the not-knowingness and curiosity that are present when our minds come into a state of wonder naturally flows through us when our surroundings are new. It's not so much the distance that you travel, but it's that quality of attentiveness and openness to new experiences that allows you to actually encounter the forces of that journey. Encounter means "to meet," and you can't meet something if you aren't present. It is when you are on a journey that you may encounter yourself through whatever internal resources you have to draw on to flow with your experience.

A day trip is an easy and affordable way to get spacious, switch up the routine from daily life, and come into a state of wonder. You can encounter new surroundings and allow them to call forth the parts of yourself that thrive in those surroundings. You can feel that internal change and learn from it, and then come home, with renewed knowledge and wisdom to flow with in your own life and to share with those around you.

We do this all the time without realizing it. Think of the last time you went to the grocery store. Perhaps you went when it wasn't crowded, and you were able to mosey through the aisles, find what you needed, maybe even picked up a few fun new foods, and then used what you found there to cook a meal that nourished you and your family. Or maybe you went when it was as packed as an anthill, and you felt frustrated and crowded as you rushed through the aisles, unable to locate a few things on your list, and you left in a poor mood, came home, and felt annoyed by everyone.

We always bring back what we think we have learned, and that energy reverberates within us and is shared with the people around us through our behavior. All journeys bring us back to ourselves if we let them. While we can choose to make every moment an adventure, the context of a day trip is enough of a pattern-interruption that we might find ourselves more easily aligned with our innate curiosity and ability to play with life.

When you return home from your day trip, pause. Take a few moments to notice or journal about the gifts or deeper noticing that you brought back. When we leave the familiar, we come home to ourselves. We allow the external changes to help us turn toward the unchanging core self within.

## Journal Contemplations

+ How can you share the expansiveness from your journey with the people around you?
+ When you travel, what is it that allows you to come into a state of wonder?
+ What internal conditions do you need to cultivate in order to be open to curiosity?

# 52

## Begin to see that everything that happens to you is there to help you learn

"Experience is the best teacher of all. And for that, there are
no guarantees that one will become an artist. Only the journey
matters."
—*Harry Callahan*

L ife gets a lot more interesting when you start asking yourself, "What can I learn from this experience?" It is easy
to push against life, to get attached to the joy of the high points and
the pain of the low points, ping-ponging between acceptance and
resistance of the circumstances that arise and the way we feel about
those circumstances. But what if we stopped pushing and realized
that everything that happens has been given to us for our ultimate
fulfillment and freedom? Consider this: your greatest losses serve
you. They show you how you are identified with the changeable, and
the pain of loss creates an opening for you to connect more deeply to
the supreme reality, that which never changes. Your greatest joys can

teach you about that Self-illumined light within, which is brighter than even the highest joy you have ever experienced. The times in your life that are more even keeled usher you into stillness, giving you the space to feel the pull of the divine within, which wants to be seen and experienced.

When you choose to relate to life this way, you begin to come home to yourself with more ease. My experience has been that I have mistaken my home for something outside of myself—a lover, a parent, a job, a situation, an experience. I've used all of these in the past as markers that I could point to as evidence that I was worthy, that I had a place in the world, that I mattered. The process of losing the external things that I thought conferred upon me a measure of worth led first to a boatload of pain. Pain led me to deepen my practice, and practice gave me a sense of peace when my mind got quiet enough to hear the call to come home. I grew to see that my worth was never outside of me. The feeling of mattering and of having a place where I was always welcome, meant that all of those things I sought were intrinsic, inherent, and already mine. The experiences were there for me to wake up to feeling the home inside, the one that can never be taken away, the home I carried within before I could remember and will continue to even when I forget.

At different junctures in life, I hope you have experienced divine consciousness, a sense of expansive awareness marked by peacefulness that is beautiful, and that you can relax into and be nourished. This is your birthright as a human. Everything around you is there to help you realize either that peace or the obstacles to that peace that you can remove or relate to differently. Everything around you is sent to help you know—without a doubt and completely—that you are home.

# Journal Contemplations

* When you ask, "What can I learn from this?" is it easier to be present with your life?
* What themes for possible learning arise?
* Are you more at home with yourself when you see experience as a gift rather than a burden?

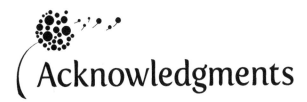

# Acknowledgments

*T*his book would not be possible without the love and support of family and friends, teachers, and spirit! Thank you to the divine in the form of creativity, which inspired this book and gave me the energy to see it through to completion. Thank you to my father, Carmichael Taylor, who has always been my biggest supporter and my greatest teacher. Thank you to my stepmom, Althea Danzey, for your loving care and support. Thank you to Rod Stryker for your amazing teachings through ParaYoga, which brightened the fire in my belly and set me on a path of returning to myself. Thank you to Pandit Rajmani Tigunait, PhD, for sharing the most auspicious teachings and for doing so with such love, joy, and kindness. The Himalayan Institute will always be my spiritual home. Thank you to Kathryn Templeton for imparting your wisdom and knowledge of Ayurveda, which returned to me my ability to heal. Thank you to Kathlyn Hendricks for sharing the science of body intelligence, presencing, and pathways back to essence. My time with you in LAT was transformative beyond belief.

Thank you to my trusted readers: Althea Danzey, Carmichael Taylor, Ambrose Crenshaw, Lauren Geschel, Ali Green, Scarlett McCahill, Laurel Peterson, Tracee Stanley, and Kathlyn Hendricks. Your feedback and support was invaluable.

Thank you to my husband, Ambrose Crenshaw, for your love, presence, and consistent encouragement. You are #crenshawesome.

CPSIA information can be obtained
at www.ICGtesting.com
Printed in the USA
BVHW03s2054160918
527656BV00001B/9/P